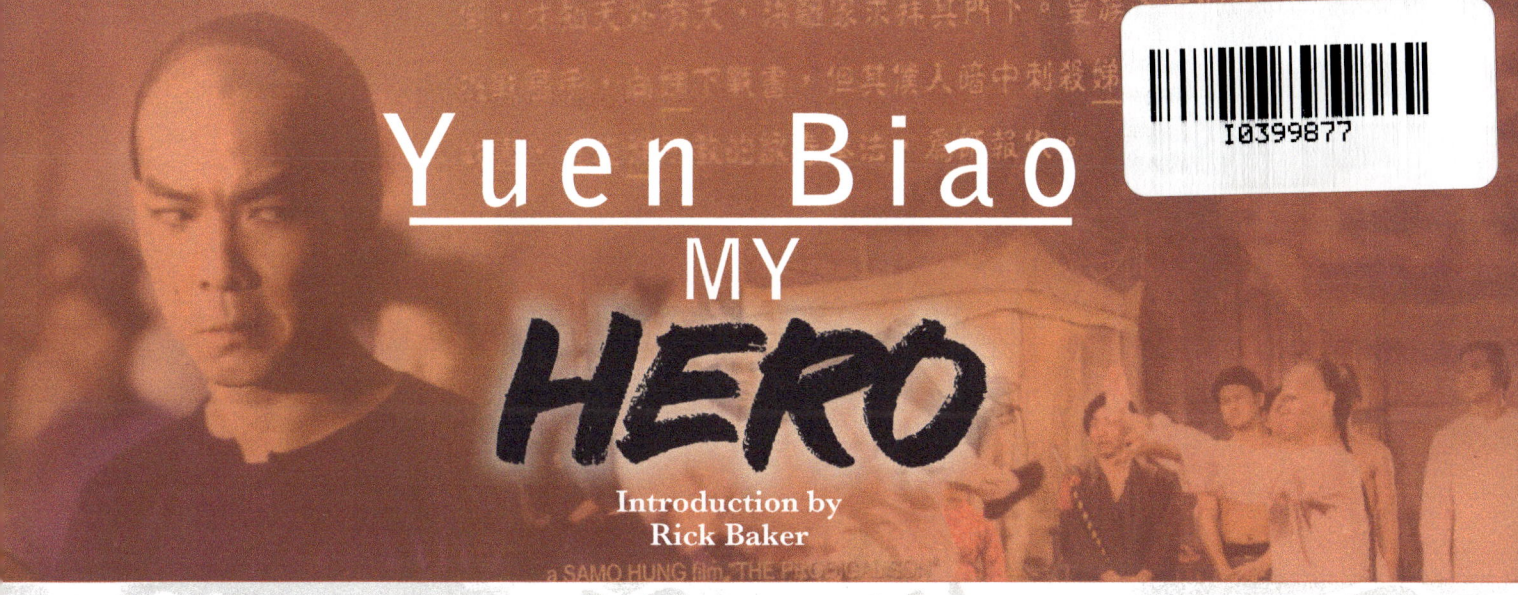

Yuen Biao
MY HERO

Introduction by Rick Baker

Welcome to this special issue dedicated to Yuen Biao. As part of our Eastern Heroes special, we are excited to feature one of Hong Kong cinema's most legendary action heroes. In the mid-90s, we were fortunate enough to interview Yuen Biao at Sammo Hung's offices during a production meeting for "Don't Give a Damn." Despite his limited English, Yuen was open to being interviewed and shared some fascinating stories, including one about calling on his "Big Brother" Sammo to retrieve a 20-cent debt from a young Jackie Chan during their days at the Peking Opera School.

Although Yuen Biao never quite achieved the same level of international fame as his "Three Dragons" co-stars, Sammo Hung and Jackie Chan, his impact on Hong Kong cinema cannot be denied. Films such as "Prodigal Son," "Knockabout," and "Magnificent Butcher" showcased his impressive talents, but it was his collaborations with Sammo and Jackie in the 80s that truly cemented his place in cinematic history.

However, in the 90s, Yuen seemed to have lost some of his previous success, despite continuing to make movies and TV series. In this issue, we take a deep dive into his films from the 90s, which are often overlooked, in an effort to promote this legendary action hero and revive interest in his work. With boutique labels re-mastering some of his classics, a whole new audience is discovering Yuen's incredible talent.

For me, Yuen Biao has been a personal icon and source of inspiration, and I am honored to dedicate this issue to him. From his breath taking acrobatic stunts to his iconic kick off the crate in "Twinkle Twinkle" Yuen has given us countless hours of entertainment and joy. We hope that this issue will help to pay tribute to his legacy and continue to inspire a new generation of fans.

Credits

Rick baker: Editor in Chief
Front Cover Artwork: Darren Wheeling
Designed By Tim Hollingsworth

Contributors

Paul Bramhill
Mike Nesbitt
Simon Pritchard
Alan Donkin
Matt Routledge
Shazard Asghar

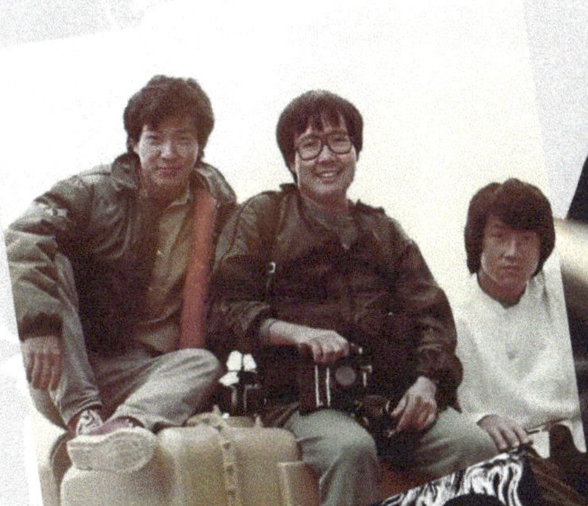

FILM REVIEWS BY JUSTYN HUGHES

西藏小子 (1992)
A Kid From Tibet
HK$ Box Office: 10,384,155
Yuen Biao productions LTD

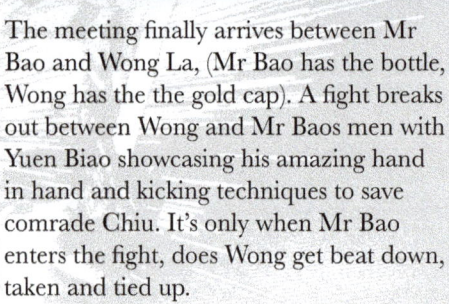

In His first and final movie has Director, A kid From Tibet sees Yuen Biao play Wong La, a Tibetan monk who has gained spiritual powers through years of training. Never seeing the outside world, Wong is asked to visit Hong Kong in seek of the Babu Gold Bottle, A treasure of the temple.

First, he heads out in search of someone who could help him get closer to finding the gold bottle, Comrade Chiu, played by the beautiful Michelle Reis (Fong Sai Yuk). But unbeknown to Wong, Mr. Bao is also searching for the good cap to complete the process, played my master villain himself Yuen Wah (Iceman Cometh). Along with Nina Li Chi (Twin Dragons), they both set out to find it and will kill anyone who steps in their way.

When Wong heads to Comrade Chiu's hotel, he notices a gang trying to kill her, so he fights the gang off and saves her. They head out to Hong Kong in search of the gold bottle, when in airport, watch out for the blink and you'll miss cameo from Jackie Chan in a yellow jacket.

Sadly for Wong and chiu, they are arrested and taken to the police station and put behind bars. Here we are treated to a fun scene, as Wong showcases some of his spiritual powers and squeezes through the bars leaving the officer inside the cell.

After Wong humiliates Chiu at a party (no fault of his own) the pair end up apart and it's now that the movie really starts to pick up. Hot on his heels is Nina Li Chi, sent to get the gold cap Wong has (the missing piece for the bottle). Starting off by trying to seduce Wong, she finds out quickly he his a monk who will stick to his principles and can't be turned. This is when they fight it out, using a long whip to throw him about, this is when Biao quickly takes the lead and lands some nice kicks too fend off the attack. The scene ends with an explosion and Nina escaping empty handed.

The meeting finally arrives between Mr Bao and Wong La, (Mr Bao has the bottle, Wong has the the gold cap). A fight breaks out between Wong and Mr Baos men with Yuen Biao showcasing his amazing hand in hand and kicking techniques to save comrade Chiu. It's only when Mr Bao enters the fight, does Wong get beat down, taken and tied up.

This leads us to the finale, the two great Peking opera brothers going toe to toe, fist to fist and sword to sword delivering us a great fight scene filled with high tempo choreography, explosions and magic. In my opinion, this is the third best fight between both actors.

Kid From Tibet isn't Yuen Biao's best movie, but it's certainly a fun movie. It doesn't have action every few minutes, but that's ok, as the scenes with Yuen and Michelle are a fun watch and Yuen Wah always delivers in the villain role he does so well.

A few other fights between Yuen Biao and Yuen Wah include movies such as Iceman Cometh, Kick boxer, Eastern Condors and Portrait Of A Nymph. I hope in the future, we get to see a better quality release of this movie, maybe Eureka could do something with this; a Blu Ray would be very welcome.

布面俾 (1995)
Don't Give A Damn
Box Office: HK $5,085,770

In 1995, Don't Give A Damn was to reunite the three dragons, Jackie Chan, Sammo Hung and Yuen Biao. I believe Jackie Chan was working on other movies at the time, so the movie went ahead with Takeshi Kaneshiro in that role.

Don't Give A Damn was also controversial in the way some language was used in the movie and also the "blacking up" scenes, (which we will come too later), had issues when seen in international markets.

Sammo Hung plays Police inspector Pierre Lau, who along with Tang Chuen-shek (Takeshi Kaneshiro), are to take down drug Lord "Nakamura". During this scene, we are introduced too Officer Rambo Wong (Yuen Biao), who has a street style attitude and gets himself into trouble with his short temper. Arresting Nakamura, brings out Yamamoto (Kevin Siu), who asks one of his men to bring over some guys to make a big hit of a police station where drugs are stashed. One of the guys to come over is Martial Artist and movie director, Robert "Bobby" Samuels (who also worked with Sammo on the movie Gambling Ghost).

During this time, we have a few love interests popping up with Sammo and Biao having young ladies in their life Yau Ching (Kathy Chow) and May (Annabelle Lau).

Some of these scenes do tend to drag a little and you don't really care too much about their relationships.

A good moment is when Sammo Hung and Yuen Biao are having an argument in the police station locker room. Biao thinks he has been set up when trying to catch a gang and Sammo doesn't take lightly too that and the pair begin to fight. Both get the better of each other, blending in some nice comedy especially when Yuen Biao attempts to pick Sammo up and gets squashed beneath him.

One of my favourite scenes in the movie is the attack at the police station. First, they are delivered a parcel which blows up in the offices after being told bombs were inside. A second bomb goes off sending everyone into a frenzy, a team of bomb experts arrive and tells everyone to evacuate. Pierre and Tang go back inside to check what's happening and realise quickly, not all is what it seems. A big shoot out occurs, Pierre takes on one of the gang (Robert Samuels), a toe to toe fight until they get away and escape into a van.

Note the scene above when the gang escaped, shows Robert Samuels performing a stunt all in one take running, jumping over a fence and then into the moving van. Robert was told before this scene, if he can make it in one take, he will be part of the stunt team moving forward. Robert did the take and the rest is history.

When Pierre's girl is kidnapped in a car by gun point by the gang, the scene that follows is brought a lot of attention, especially in the west. Here, we see Yuen Biao and Takeshi Kaneshiro (Black up), trying to disguise themselves as black guys to enter the gangs hideout. This has had many mixed reactions over the years and some even say, was a reason Jackie Chan may not have done the movie (but I think that was just filming schedules). Robert Samuels said this about the movie in an old interview I did with him for Asian Movie Pulse.

"Sammo built that film around me. There were some issues about the Screenplay and one scene had racial overtones. Sammo had nothing to do with that, it was the screenwriter and me who constantly battled over the script".

This leads us onto the finale, Sammo, Biao, Collin Chou, Robert Samuels, Kelvin Wong Siu, Roy Filler, Habby Heske, the list continues. A gritty showdown between each group, Yuen Biao does well, but I don't feel his character is given enough time to shine during the fight sequences, especially in the finale. We do get to see a good 3 way fight between Sammo, Collin and Robert with some nice camera angels flowing in and out of the action. Also leave the end credits running, as it shows the cast and crew celebrating the final scene of the movie.

Overall, "Don't Give A Damn" has its moments. Some good action sequences, enjoyed the fights, but could have been better. If they spent less time focusing on the relationships and added a few more action sequences, we could have had a better result.

馬永貞 (1997)
Hero
Box Office: HK $3,015,240
Directed by Corey Yuen (Righting Wrongs)

Hero is a 1997 remake of the Shaw Brothers classic "Boxer From Shantung". The movie focuses mainly on the character Ma Wing Ching, played by Takeshi Kaneshiro, as he rises to the top of society, but encounters many troubles along the way. Late 1800's in Shantung, many people were hungry due to droughts, leaving their homes and heading into Shanghai (which was under British jurisdiction). Ma Wing Ching and his brother, played by Yuen Wah, head out looking for work at the pier but find themselves stuck in manual Labour. Until big time gangster arrives called Tam Sei (Yuen Biao), a person Ma Wing Ching wants to be, powerful, has money and territory to go with the status. Tam Sei Lays down a challenge to Ma, capture his expensive pocket watch and it's all his. This leads us to a quick sequence with both fighting on a running horse, both getting the better of each other, ending in a draw. (This earns Ma respect from Tam). The two brothers then get a job at Tams nightclub, where they meet Yim Yeung Tin (Valerie Chow) which Ma quickly falls for. Whilst there, he meets a singer called Kam, who quickly falls in love with Ma, after a fight breaks out and he protects her. As time moves on, we see Ma and his brother doing small robberies for money, Ma and the relationship with singer Kam is moving along, but the night he promises to take her on a date, he gets arrested and the meeting doesn't happen. Afterwards, a meeting between local crime bosses Tam and Yeung (Yuen Tak) doesn't go to well, with Tam laying the law down and threatening Yeung not to step on his turf again. This leads to Yeung getting help from the cops, allowing his men to try and kill Tam when he leaves the building.

This scene is very well done, with Yuen Biao displaying his excellent kicking skills, his character having to fend off an axe attack before nearly being killed himself. (Saved by Ma Wing Ching). I have to also mention the colour and feel of the scene, the street lamps giving it a certain feel with the blue tint and mist, works very well with the action taking place.

The two crime bosses are becoming more involved in each other's turfs, with Ma

Wing Ching pushing more to take over a few himself and be more involved with Tam Se. During this time, Ma is now involved with beauty Yim Yeung Tin and has been drinking a lot more, not paying a lot of attention to those around him. He dismisses Tam Se and even his brother to stay along side Yim, something he would later regret. One evening Ma Wing Ching is attacked and his badly beaten, stabbed and thrown over the side of a bridge and left for dead. This is a fantastic sequence filled with tension, hard hitting action and lots of great stunt work. Master Tam is told about this and rushes out to help Ma, but once at the scene, quickly realises it's a set up and that Ma has already been killed (unknowing to them, Ma was found and taken to safety).

Here Boss Yeung attacks Tam, leading to Tam being stabbed and shot in the leg. Tam is then seen being taken to a shooting range and executed. So with Tam and Ma out the way, Boss Yeung sets his sights on becoming the main boss of Shanghai. The finale of this movie, is all out action. We have suicide bombers, cannons being fired, machine guns and some awesome hand to hand combat. Ma Wing Ching turns up with the coffin of Tam for Boss Yeung Inauguration; Yeung doesn't like this and sends in the cops to deal with the situation. This is when all hell breaks lose, Yeungs men and the police Vs Ma Wing Ching and his crew. During this sequence, Boss Tams coffin opens up with Tam coming up to shoot a few guns, leaving Yeung in disarray. (A very cool looking Yuen Biao, with a cigar in his mouth).

Ma Wing Ching is hurt, leaving the two Peking opera brothers to fight it out, Yuen Biao Vs Yuen Tak. Great hand to hand combat with both bosses battling it out to be number 1. This is a violent scene, which leaves lots of blood spilled and a nasty ending (just how we like it).

Being a remake of a Shaw Brothers classic, it will always be compared to the original. Is this better than Boxer From Shantung? The answer is no. Does Hero have some great moments throughout the movie? Yes. Overall, this isn't a classic but it does have enough to make this a good movie. I feel it needed a few more action sequences, a few of the scenes kind of pass you by, but the action does make up for that.

Good performances from the main cast, Corey Yuen I feel did a good job directing and for its time, great seeing Yuen Biao given a big role again.

If you haven't bought this movie yet, look at investing in the 88 Films release, looks awesome on Blu Ray.

黃飛鴻之鬼腳七 (1993)
Kickboxer
Box Office: HK $7,606,886
Directed By: Wu Ma
Action By: Yuen Biao

After his experience working on the movie "Once Upon A Time In China" and feeling let down with his screen time and lack of fight scenes, Yuen Biao went onto make Kickboxer. This was the movie where he wanted to show the audience he can still fight with the best of them and he certainly shown this here.

Kickboxer opens inside a pawn shop, where people can sell their goods for money. But in the background, they are preparing to gain more opium and to get people hooked on it too fed there habits. Gold Panther, a cop, arrives in order to arrest those responsible, which then turns into a fight sequence which really sets the tone for the rest of the movie. Gold Panther (with his gold plated shoes) takes most of them down, apart from one who manages to escape.

On his way back from his travels, Lau Zhai (Yuen Biao) and his college Ah So (Wu Ma), bump into an old friend "Ming" on a boat (played by Tai Bo). Whilst exploring the boat, the pair bump into a female reporter from Shanghai and form a quick bond. The scene which follows shows a sign saying no Chinese allowed in the dining area, to which Lau Zhai confronts the doorman and a big fight breaks loose. Yuen Biao here brings out all the moves, high kicks, hand to hand combat, flips and even has ago at "snake style", but it doesn't help him much. A fantastic scene, one I've watched many times over the years. We quickly move on to meeting the chairman and main villain of this movie, chairman Wah (Yuen Wah). He has gathered various leaders to dinner, whilst talking; he takes out a pistol and shoots one in the back of the head. Now we head over to Po Chi Lam, where Lau Zhai has brought back presents for everyone then finds out Master Wong Fei Hung has gone travelling.

When eating in the evening and a few too many drinks, the group head back to Po Chi Lam, unaware inside are a group of masked intruders hiding in the shadows. They nearly go undetected until Lau heads into a corner and starts to take a wee, straight onto one of their faces. A funny

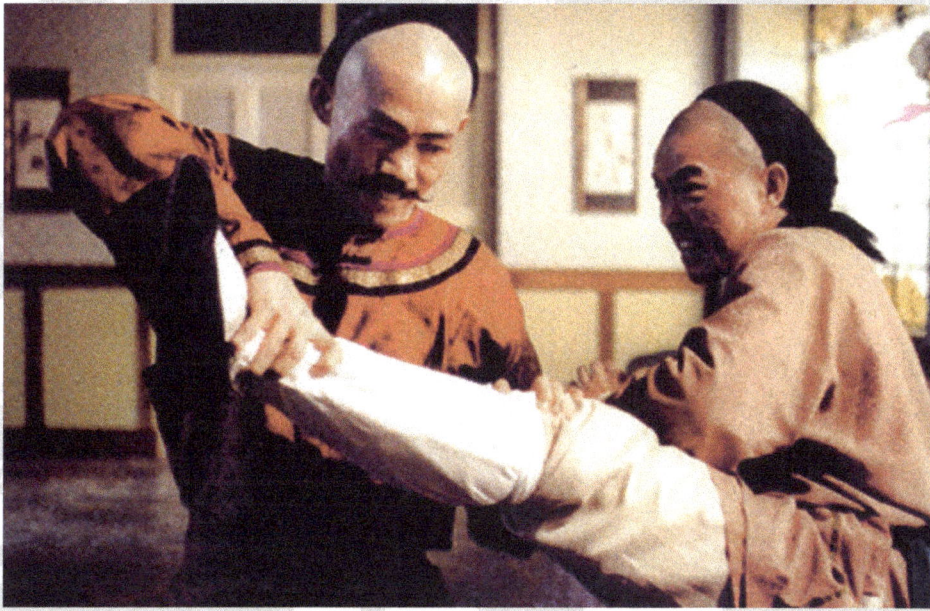

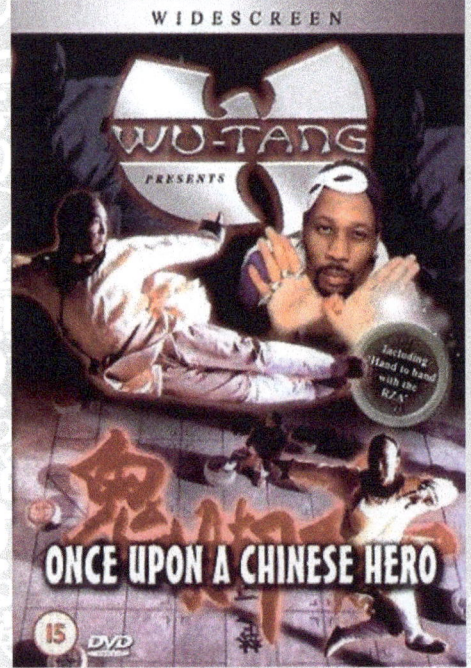

scene which makes me laugh each time. It's then Po Chi Lam Vs the masked intruders, each character having their own opponents do deal with and what we get is a great fight sequence. Yuen Biao showcasing some nice leg techniques, flips and close combat movements to defeat his opponent, showing the audience he his still on top of his game.

Lau meets up in his old friend Ming in a tea house, shortly after Ming is taken into the back, so Lau follows to see what is happening. He quickly discovers an opium den, beats up his old friend, but then is quickly attacked by multiple opponents. Shortly after Chairman Wah arrives and quickly fights off Lau and quickly let's everyone know, who's the boss. Afterwards Lau is told to leave Po Chi Lam for causing to much trouble, he leaves and ends up facing off against Gold Panther. Making a plan, Lau goes to chairman Wah with Ming and helps save Wah when a gun is pulled on him. This is to get Wah to trust him, so he can find out what's going on inside his organisation and give the details to Gold Panther. This results in opium being found and set alight by Gold Panther in front of chairman Wah and his men.

Following this we get to witness the biggest game of chess ever made, a giant chess board drawn on the floor with big pieces to move around. This is a very entertaining scene and always great viewing for the audience. Chairman Wah, Lau and his men have gathered to move opium from there hideout, but Officer Gold Panther arrives to arrest them but doesn't end well for him at all. Once facing Wah and his

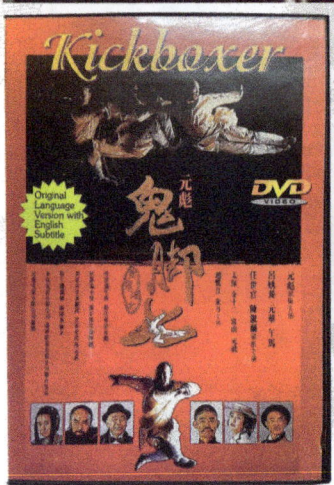

men, Gold Panther is hung up with ropes in the air, alcohol thrown onto him and set alight. Lau arrives to late and watches on as gold Panther is burning. The finale! What can I say about the finale of this movie, other than it's awesome. Yuen Biao really does get to shine here, arriving at chairman Wahs, taking on a few of his men with some excellent kicks and acrobatic movements, then facing off against Chang Shan. A hard hitting face off which ends with Yuen Biao delivering a spin kick which leaves you mouth open, wondering how he did that. Then it's time for the big showdown, as the two Peking opera brothers face off in a fight to the death, Yuen Wah using the eagle technique, to perfection with great sound effects to add more to the scene. Both guys delivering performances from the past, two legends showing the audience how a good fight scene is put together. Also in this scene, we get to see the ghost leg. A third leg which appears during their fight as Biao lands a kick which Yuen Wah isn't expecting and wonders how it happened (A nice touch).

Overall, Kickboxer is a good movie taking us back to the 70's to early 80's Kung fu movies. If it wasn't for the experience Yuen Biao had on" Once Upon A Time In China", would Kickboxer ever had been made? Everything happens for a reason and I'm very happy this movie was made, for sure, one of the better Yuen Biao's better movies from the 90's. And in my opinion one of the last great performances given by Yuen Biao in a traditional Kung Fu role.

Kickboxer needs the Blu Ray treatment; this is a movie which needs a proper release, one to check out for sure.

黃飛鴻 (1991)
Once Upon a Time in China
Box Office: HK $$29,672,278

Once Upon A Time In China was the revival of the legendary folk hero Wong Fei Hung. Many say this was the movie which started the craze again for period kung fu movies, which were fading out after the success of the "Modern Day" Martial Art films throughout the 80's onwards. The movie also won Best film at the HK movie awards, along with best action, best original score and best editing.

Directed by Tsui Hark (Peking Opera Blues), we follow the story of Wong Fei Hung (Jet Li), in the late 19th century Foshan China. Running his medicine clinic "Po Chi Lam" along with his three students Porky, Bucktooth So and Kai. Wong meets "13th Aunt", played by Rosamund Kwan, you can see she instantly has feelings for Wong and something which gets explored more throughout the series of movies.

An opera troupe arrive in Foshan for some performances, here we meet Leung Foon (Yuen Biao), a mischievous character who has some problems with a local gang and also wants to become a student of Wong Fei Hung. One morning, Foon is confronted by gang leader (Yau Gin Gwok) and asks Foon to chop of his own hand as a gift. Foon decides that isn't going to happen and challenges the leader to a fight, but instead is attack by a few of his men with Foon (Yuen Biao) performing an excellent backflip, followed by a spinning kick to escape. It's a shame Leung Foon and the gang leader didn't have a one on one fight, as Yau Gin Gwok did an excellent job with The South Shaolin Master movies. To be honest, that is probably Yuen Biaos only big chance to

shine in this movie and it's over in seconds. Don't get me wrong, he does have other fight scenes in this movie, but doesn't get the chance to showcase his true ability on screen.

This leads on to a big fight sequence between Leung Foon, the gang and Wong Fei Hungs student Porky in the market. The fight ends up inside the restaurant where Wong Fei Hung is discussing dealings with the British. Wong Fei Hung quickly defeats the intruders, with Jet Li showcasing some nice kicks. (He doesn't do many in this movie due to breaking his leg).

Meanwhile, Leung Foon meets a northern martial artist who has come into town called "Iron Vest" (Yen Shi Kwan). Foon sees him begging for money and thinks no more of it, until one night Iron Vest is challenged to a duel with Yeung Chung Yan. The scenery looks great, with a big burning fire and both guys throwing down in front of it, until Yeung is defeated and Iron Vest improves his status in the martial world.

One of the big scenes which stood out to me was the Peking opera performance and attack on Wong Fei Hung and the audience.

Here we get to see Wong and his students fight not only the intruders but also the police, who are shooting and killing innocent people. Jet Li had broken his leg by now; so much of the action was performed by doubles, barring a few moves here and there for the rest of the movie. This was another moment where Yuen Biao was massively under used, why he wasn't given more time to shine in this fight sequences was beyond me. (Maybe they didn't want Jet Li out shinning?).

Another great fight scene was between Jet Li and Yen Shi Kwan (Fearless Hyena). Wong Fei Hung is challenged in his clinic, Leung Foon has teamed up with Iron Vest but doesn't like that he's there with him to challenge Wong Fei Hung. After this, Iron Vest leaves and joins the Shaho Gang and even though Leung Foon rejects the morals of the gang, also joins. The gang takes 13th Aunt has hostage along with BuckTooth and keep them locked away, waiting for Wong Fei Hung to arrive. Wong and his students disguise themselves and get into the gangs hideout, on a ship.

The end fight scene is one of the movies highlights, Wong Fei Hung Vs Iron Vest with Leung Foon and others helping out also. I didn't care much for the big ladder fight with Wong and Iron Vest flying around everywhere and felt like it was wasting time. If Jet Li hasn't broken his leg, I felt this scene would have been much better with more grounded fight work.

I have to say again, Yuen Biao was criminally under used throughout this film, in terms of the fight scenes alone. We know before filming, his character was to be the main focus of the movie, until that was changed and the focus went onto Jet Li (Wong Fei Hung). Yuen Biao wasn't happy about this and of course went on to make Kickboxer just show Tsui Hark and others he was still the real deal.

Overall, Once Upon A Time In China is a good, enjoyable movie. It does have its flaws like Jet Li being doubled throughout due to his leg break and Yuen Biao not being used enough. But still I can find time to rewatch once in a while.
Is it a classic? Not for me. A good watch, but to be a classic you have to be on par with movies such as The Prodigal Son, Magnificent Butcher and beyond.

Once Upon A Time In China followed on with 5 sequels, Jet Li playing in 4 of them with Vincent Zhao in parts 4-5.

新碧血劍 (1993)
Sword Stained With Royal Blood

The Sword Stained with Royal Blood seems to be a movie which completely goes under the radar. Directed by Larry Cheung (Devils Vendetta) and action by Brandy Yuen (part of the famous Yuen clan), Sword Stained with Royal Blood is a surprisingly good Wu Xia movie.

The movie opens with a big battle to kill all eunuchs, as they believe to have set up secret police units. This is led by Melvin Wong and Peter Chan (cameos), as the audience is treated to a few limbs being cut off, high paced action, just what you expect from Wu Xia movie. Danny Lee appears as the "Golden Snake Man" and showcases his powerful skills throughout the movie.

Yuen Biao plays Constable Yuen Shing Chi, who ends up bound together with Kau (Sharla Cheung Man). After he arrests her for being a bandit, they are attacked on their travels by Ho, a member of the poison sector. I have to say this is a fun, imaginative scene with people flying through the trees, flying up from under the ground to attack and a magical harp which fires when played to certain tunes.

We are then introduced too Master Woo Hark (Shut Bo Wa), speaking to a number of martial art leaders have gathered. They are hiding away from the Golden Snake man, who said will arrive by full moon, but constable Yuen arrives and a nice, quick fire fight scene breaks out. Yuen Biao does well in these type of movies, shame he didn't make many more of these afterwards.

Constable Yuen finds himself face on with the golden snake man, who is looking to kill his prisoner Kau. As lightning strikes, the noise sends Snake Man into a frenzy, and attacks constable Yuen with anger and force. But both come together and start to form a bond, respecting each other's skills in the martial art world. He gives constable Yuen a dagger and goes in his way, leaving Yuen and Kau to move along and find a Mr Wen (Elvis Tsui), the leader of the world of martial arts.

A fight breaks out between different secs, Yuen Biao and Elvis bringing the audience some nice choreography, with pulse racing music, delivers us a good moment in the movie. The main goal is to own the Golden

Serpent Sword and a martial arts manual which will make you invincible.

The movie moves along at a nice pace with Lots of great scenes, including many fight scenes to keep any martial arts/Wu Xia fan happy. One of the highlights is the battle between Yuen Biao and Danny Lee, where snake man explains he will kill the constable in less than 3 strikes, if not, he can arrest him. During the fight, snake man drinks some wine, which has been poisoned, but not by constable Yuen.

After a few more sword battles, smoke bombs and flying through trees, we are treated to an all out finale with constable Yuen, Mr Wen and master Wu going blade to blade, kick to kick and blood for blood. The scenery is awesome, starting off inside a cave, lightening bolts coming from the swords, flying about and rocks exploding, pushes the scene along at a good pace. Then smashing there way out of the cave, we see an arm sliced off, and a body cut in two. A satisfying ending to a good movie.

I have to say, after rewatching this movie, I enjoyed it more than I remember. Ok, this isn't a big budget movie of it's time, overshadowed by others of its time such as Moon Warriors, Blade Of Fury too name but a few. But it does have a ton of sword fights, some great characters and a good finale. The story does wonder off at times, but that I can forgive that as I enjoy the rest of the movie. It isn't a classic, but it's also

under rated and I feel a good future release of this movie, could gain more of a fan base. One to check out.

Once Upon a Time in the 90's
A Retrospective of His Most Overlooked Decade
By Paul Bramhall
(cityonfire.com/author)

There would be few out there who'd argue that, in the world of kung Fu cinema, the names of Jackie Chan, Sammo Hung, and Yuen Biao will forever be imprinted. Collectively known as the Three Dragons, between them, the trio have headlined some of the defining movies of the genre, and even more when you count their experience behind the camera. Having studied at the same Peking Opera school under the tutelage of Yu Jim-Yuen, it was during the 1980's that their popularity sky-rocketed, and throughout the decade they'd appear on the big screen together a total of 6 times. It was Project A, Meals on Wheels, and Dragons Forever that became the defining moments of their shared outings (with the other 3 being entries in Sammo Hung's Lucky Stars comedy franchise), with the latter continuing to be the final time they shared the screen as of the time of writing. Part of this was down to a well-documented underlying tension during the filming of Dragons Forever.

By this point Jackie Chan and Sammo Hung had both become goliaths in the world of Hong Kong action cinema, and the mutual collaboration of their earlier productions had here turned into something more like a professional rivalry (which was ironically a win for the audience, as their respective stunt teams attempted to outdo each other in the fall heavy finale!). As a result Yuen Biao, the youngest and most passive of the trio, often feels like he's side-lined in the final product, a feeling which was echoed by his own opinions towards the production. By the time the 90's rolled around Jackie and Sammo's careers followed the expected paths. Jackie began to aggressively target the U.S. market, first with limited success thanks to 1995's Rumble in the Bronx, and then striking box office gold with 1998's Rush Hour, kicking off a string of Hollywood starring vehicles. Comparatively Sammo had a tumultuous decade due to the highly publicised divorce of his first wife, starring in a string of hard-hitting contemporary actioners (often with questionable humor), before he also headed stateside in 1998 to headline the TV show Martial Law. Yuen Biao on the other hand seemed to become a little

lost in the 1990's, perhaps missing the close collaboration of his Peking Opera brothers combined with shifting audience's tastes, his filmography for the decade is a curious mix of genres and oddities which saw him work in a number of countries. Many seem to write the 90's off when it comes to discussing Biao's best work, painting the decade with a broad brushstroke of low budget actioners, and some even saying he was past his physical prime. Considering Biao was still the spritely age of 33 in 1990, an age when Jackie Chan was directing and starring in Project A II, and Sammo Hung was similarly directing and starring in My Lucky Stars, such observations seem unjustly harsh. Sure nobody was expecting him to be a human rubber band like he was in his late 70's work like Knockabout, but his kung fu brothers had already proven that a Hong Kong action stars expiry date doesn't finish at 30. So were the 90's really as bad to Biao as the decade's reputation would have us believe, or is it just a misunderstood era in the youngest dragon's filmography? In this feature, we'll delve into the most overlooked decade of Biao's career in a quest to find out.

In 1990 we got a triple dose of Biao, clocking in what would be his busiest year of the decade. The year can almost be taken as a microcosm of the decade as a whole – some trash, some gold. Let's start with the trash. Similar to Jackie Chan, possibly even more so, Biao had built up a hugely popular fanbase in Japan. I mean this guy even released an album there during the 80's. Biao had already started to capitalise on his Japanese fan base with the 1989 Hong Kong-Japanese co-production The Peacock King, which saw him starring alongside the likes of Mikami Hiroshi, Yasuda Narumi, and Hidari Tompei. Featuring Biao paired up with a Japanese monk, together they have to battle against manga style monsters in order to stop The Gates of Hell from opening, and the result proved to be a hit at the Japanese box office. A sequel was rushed into production, and in 1990 it hit the screens in the form of Saga of the Phoenix. While The Peacock King was a fun fantasy with entertaining effects work, the sequel is a miserable disaster on almost every level. Not that it can really be blamed on Biao – he spends almost the entire movie frozen in a block of ice, only really showing up to do anything significant in the finale, however his appearance was enough to be used as the star in the promotional material. Even Mikami Hiroshi who played the monk in the original had enough sense not to return for the sequel, so instead his character is replaced by Abe Hiroshi in an early role, who thankfully would go onto do much better things later in his career. Unbelievably the sequel also features Zatoichi himself, Shintaro Katsu. Awful in every sense of the word, if there's a movie to avoid in Biao's entire filmography, then it's Saga of the Phoenix. Thankfully he bounced back almost immediately thanks to re-teaming with Sammo Hung in Teddy Kwan's Shanghai Shanghai. This would be the first time for him to share the screen with his big brother since 1988's Dragons Forever, and you can feel the difference in energy emanating off the screen when compared to that movie I choose to no longer mention. Other Seven Little Fortunes alumni are also onboard, with Corey Yuen on choreography duty (having worked with Biao on the previous decades Righting Wrongs and Eastern Condors) and Yuen Tak in a small supporting role. Here Biao's role plays to his strengths, a humble country bumpkin who comes to the big city, and his resulting run-ins with a triad gang led by Sammo Hung leads to a satisfying final fight between the pair. It's good enough to forgive Kwan's messy narrative during the rest of the movie that often feels like it's not sure what it's supposed to be, however Biao anchors proceedings well, and is surrounded by legends like Anita Mui for him to play off. Shanghai Shanghai's selling point will always be the Biao vs Sammo fight though, going at it for the first time since their brief scuffle 4 years earlier in Millionaire's Express. While in that one their fight was a misunderstanding, here they go at each other as full-fledged enemies, and it's a suitably high impact throw down with Biao looking dapper in a tailored suit.

The pair would meet again on screen throughout the years, including a locker room scuffle the next time they'd reunite in 1995's Don't Give a Damn (which we'll get to), but nothing would match the quality of their fight in Shanghai Shanghai. Rounding out 1990 is my personal favourite Biao flick of the 90's – License to Steal. Similar to She Shoots Straight which hit HK cinemas a few months earlier, here once more Sammo is on producer duty for what's actually a starring vehicle for his new flame Joyce Godenzi. However it's arguably Biao that steals the show whenever he's onscreen. If he felt his mentally unbalanced character from Dragons Forever got short thrift, then here director Billy Chan lets him loose as an overly zealous fan of chivalrous swordsmen from old wuxia novels, believing himself to be a modern-day incarnation of one. While he may not be on screen the whole time, whenever he is it's a joy to watch, and he gets a worthy final fight against Billy Chow, making Biao the last of the Three Dragons to go up against the Canada born kickboxer.

It was in 1991 that Biao's feelings of being side-lined reared their head once more. Signing up for Tsui Hark's Once Upon a Time in China as Wong Fei Hung's (being played by Jet Li) right-hand man, it's rumoured that Biao believed his role to be a much bigger one than what ended up onscreen. It makes sense when viewing his performance, as despite his limited screen time, whenever he is onscreen there's a distinct feeling we're watching someone who thinks they should be the star of the show. Instead, it became Jet Li's defining role and led to resurgence in the kung Fu movie with local audiences. More credence is given to the theory when we consider the fact that Biao never returned for any of the subsequent sequels, his character replaced by a more comedy inclined Max Mok, and 2 years later Biao would produce his own take on the Wong Fei Hung universe with Kickboxer (we'll get to that later as well). Perhaps feeling burnt by his experience on Once Upon a Time in China, a year later Biao decided to take matters into his own hands. The result was A Kid from Tibet. Biao starred, he produced, he directs, and he even set up his own production company (Yuen Biao Productions Ltd.) which didn't produce anything outside of this one movie. Compared to his Peking Opera brothers

Biao was decidedly late to the directing game, with Sammo Hung first directing himself in 1977's The Iron Fisted Monk, and Jackie Chan doing the same with 1979's The Fearless Hyena. Unlike Jackie and Sammo who'd go on to have successful directing careers (Sammo in particular, with Jackie limited to always directing himself), A Kid from Tibet would be Biao's first and last time directing, and watching the strangely paced and tonally inconsistent end product it's easy to understand why. All of the ingredients are there for a good movie – Tibetan locations, enlisting go-to villain Yuen Wah who Biao had memorable matchups with in the previous decades Eastern Condors and The Iceman Cometh, and we even get a brief cameo from Jackie Chan. However Biao can't quite recreate the fish out of water magic that worked so well for him in movies like The Iceman Cometh and Shanghai Shanghai, most likely a result of his own directorial limitations. Once his monk arrives in Hong Kong the pacing drags as he bickers with a local contact played by Michelle Reis, and there's just enough time between action scenes for boredom to set in, a feeling that becomes more difficult to snap out of the longer A Kid from Tibet drags on. Things

are redeemed slightly by the obligatory final fight between Biao and Wah, performed with entertainingly oversized swords, but it's not enough to make Biao's directorial debut a recommendation. 1992 proved to be a year full of surprises for Biao though, and one of the biggest ones came with the release of Ronny Yu's Shogun and Little Kitchen. Made just a year before his seminal The Bride with White Hair, Yu was only the second director (after Alfred Cheung with 1988's On the Run – arguably Biao's best movie of his entire filmography) to cast Biao in a non-fighting role. Similar to how Biao incorporated his athleticism into the sport of soccer in 1983's The Champions, here he gets to show off his acrobatics as the chef of a restaurant run by Ng Man-Tat. A feel-good Lunar New Year flick, look out for minor supporting roles from Jimmy Wang Yu and Leung Kar-Yan. Interestingly Shogun and Little Kitchen predates both Stephen Chow's God of Cookery and Jackie Chan's Mr. Nice Guy, offering up an opportunity to see Biao in a different kind of culinary role, and one that he looks to be enjoying.

As much as I could create a whole argument around how if there was no Yuen Biao, there would be no God of Cookery or Shaolin Soccer, we'll move on. Biao also banked on his Japanese connection again during the same year, being cast as an opium dealing mob boss in Setting Sun, a multi-national co-production made during the Nikkatsu studios 80th anniversary. While the thought of Yuen Biao appearing in a movie that stars Diana Lane and Donald Sutherland was an unlikely one at the time, and still feels hard to believe even today, for fans of Asian cinema the fact that he's in a movie which also features Jo Shishido will trump both of the Hollywood stars any day of the week. Taking Saga of the Phoenix (damn, I mentioned it) into consideration and Shintaro Katsu's role in that one, Biao is one of the few HK action stars who can say he's played alongside such legends of Japanese cinema. But back to Setting Sun, as entertaining as it is to see Biao in a villain role, and something I would have loved to see more of, the movie itself is a sprawling 150+ minute mess, which no amount of gorgeous set design and sweeping cinematography can compensate for. While it does offer up an opportunity for Biao to once more unleash the onscreen fighting prowess he's known for, set on a collision course with Masaya Kato playing a Japanese soldier and his Eurasian love interest played by Diana Lane, Setting Sun just has too much going on to be invested. Interestingly Rou Tomono, whose novel the movie is based on, decided to both adapt and direct the big screen adaptation himself, which would be his first and last

time in the director's chair, so at least he and Biao have that in common. As to what Nikkatsu were thinking giving such an epic project to a first-time director, that's likely to remain one of life's mysteries. By the time it was 1993 Biao decided it was time to get revenge on Tsui Hark's perceived short-changing of his role on Once Upon a Time in China, so he decided to create his own tale of a would-be student of Wong Fei Hung and go head-to-head against Once Upon a Time in China III in February. The result was Kickboxer (which sometime humorously goes under the aka of Once Upon a Time in China 6), and in the end Tsui Hark's 2nd sequel banked $27,540,561 at the box office, while Kickboxer banked $7,606,886. Thankfully box office returns aren't always indicative of quality, and under the direction of Wu Ma and his own fight choreography Kickboxer delivers the goods, just don't go in expecting anything that resembles the kind of budget that Tsui Hark was working with.

Amusingly Biao's Wong Fei Hung flick bypasses the elephant in the room of who'll play Wong Fei Hung by not having him appear at all, instead having Biao visit Po Chi Lam as a wannabe student only to discover he's away travelling. Of course here that doesn't matter, as indeed Kickboxer's main character is the wannabe student, and just because he can Biao also brings on-board the original Once Upon a Time in China antagonist in the form of Yen Shi-Kwan. Derivative as it may be, there can also be no doubt that yes – Biao makes for a worthy lead in a WFH flick – and he gives a spirited fighting performance, once more casting his go-to opponent Yuen Wah to duke it out with, as well as Chang Shan as a fierce kicking machine. A case of action surpassing budgetary limitations, Kickboxer ranks second behind License to Steal as my best Biao flick of the 90's, and he'd stick with Wu Ma as a director for the following years Circus Kids.

Before that though, 1993 was also the year Biao got in on the new wave wuxia craze, ironically kick started by Tsui Hark produced flicks like 1990's Swordsman and its subsequent sequels. Biao would star in a couple of new wave wuxia's during the 90's, the first being The Sword Stained with Royal Blood, then the following year in Deadful Melody. Out of all the movies Biao appeared in (even his Philippines shot cheapies – which we'll get to!), it seems to

I still can send you to the court

be these 2 that receive the most hate, at least when it comes to English language articles (and although it may be an assumption – by extension his western fan base). After reading some of the comments about these Biao flicks, from what I can surmise there's a whole generation of VHS collectors who, once these 2 titles were released in the likes of the U.S. and UK, were expecting traditional kung fu movies along the lines of Knockabout or The Prodigal Son.

The sight of these colourful, crazy wire work fuelled spectacles was met with disdain rather than enjoyment, which isn't exactly the movie's fault – they were made as new wave wuxia's, and new wave wuxia's are exactly what you get. To that end, The Sword Stained with Royal Blood is my third best Biao flick of the 90's, a wuxia so relentlessly energetic and creative with its action scenes that it's almost impossible not to enjoy. Impossible to comprehend maybe, with an overly packed plot as was par for the course in this genre, but you'd have to be dead to be not left jaw agape at some of the ingenuity behind the action. Helmed by 3-hit wonder Larry Cheung (ok, it's debatable if Devil's Vendetta and Virtual Recall could be classed as hits) and choreographed by Yuen Clan member Brandy Yuen, who previously directed Biao in 1983's The Champions, Biao's physical versatility allows for plenty of manic wirework insanity. The sight of these colourful, crazy wire work fuelled spectacles was met with disdain rather than enjoyment, which isn't exactly the movie's fault – they were made as new wave wuxia's, and new wave wuxia's are exactly what you get. To that end, The Sword Stained with Royal Blood is my third best Biao flick of the 90's, a wuxia so relentlessly energetic and creative with its action scenes that it's almost impossible not to enjoy. Impossible to comprehend maybe, with an overly packed plot as was par for the course in this genre, but you'd have to be dead to be not left jaw agape at some of the ingenuity behind the action. Helmed by 3-hit wonder Larry Cheung (ok, it's debatable if Devil's Vendetta and Virtual Recall could be classed as hits) and choreographed by Yuen Clan member Brandy Yuen, who previously directed Biao in 1983's The Champions, Biao's physical versatility allows for plenty of manic wirework insanity. A slightly more restrained take on the genre (although to be honest, anything would be), 1994's Deadful Melody sees Biao acting alongside the actress who practically became the face of new wave wuxia – Brigitte Lin. I always find if funny to think that Lin's first new wave wuxia flick was Swordman II from 1992, and in 1994 she retired, however in less than 3 years she managed to appear in over 10 of these movies, forever becoming associated with it. In Deadful Melody she's essentially riffing on her Invincible Asia character from Swordman II and The East is Red, and its Biao who's charged with escorting the deadly lyre she has a fondness for playing to her clans headquarters. For anyone who's familiar they'll know the type – a few plucks of the strings result in bodies exploding for any poor sap within its radius – and naturally every other clan leader is after it, leading to Biao constantly being attacked but having no idea why. While it can't be denied that Biao seems a little out of his depth acting alongside the likes of Brigitte Lin and Carina Lau, Deadful Melody still proves to be an entertaining entry in the genre. That's more than can be said for Circus Kids which rounded out Biao's 1994 output with a September release. After the entertaining Kickboxer it's understandable that he'd once more re-team with Wu Ma in the capacity of star and director, and Circus Kids has all the ingredients to create kung fu movie magic – not least the fact that his co-stars are fellow boot masters Donnie Yen and Ken Lo. Set in 1942 and

involving a circus troupe who are left jobless when the invading Japanese forces blow up their tent, Ma strikes an awkward balance between drama and action, with the former falling flat and the latter largely being derivative of superior productions. Ken Lo revealed that for the finale Ma requested he basically recreate his legendary performance from the finale of Drunken Master II (which had hit cinemas in February). Essentially playing the same character, his fight against Biao is at best underwhelming, embarrassingly copy and pasting moments from the movie that inspired it. As if that wasn't bad enough, Biao also gets to face off against Donnie Yen in an equally lacklustre confrontation, with the trifactor choreography team of Yuen Miu, Pan Yung-Sheng, and Mandy Chan Chi-Man seemingly unable to make Biao's style gel with the others. While Circus Kids certainly doesn't reach Saga of

the Phoenix levels of bad (at least here he's front and centre, which in some ways actually makes it more painful!), it's one of the undeniable duds of Biao's 90's filmography, and stands in stark contrast to the quality of work his kung fu brother Jackie Chan was cranking out at the same time. It's hard not to believe then that Biao wouldn't have been relieved when, in the following year, Sammo Hung called him up to co-star in a production he was also planning to direct under the title Don't Give A Damn. Widely believed to be the movie intended to reunite the Three Dragons once more, scheduling conflicts with Rumble in the Bronx prevented Jackie Chan from taking part. While the character most believe Chan would have played is replaced by Takeshi Kaneshiro, watching the end result it feels equally as likely that Chan perhaps turned down the opportunity, and the scheduling challenges

were more an excuse to save face. While Chan was leaning towards increasingly family friendly fare aimed at international markets, Don't Give a Damn is a depressingly misogynistic and racist affair, allegedly fuelled by Sammo's bitterness towards the industry and the amount of negative media attention his divorce had received. Comparative to some of the lines Sammo comes out with Biao escapes the production relatively unscathed; however he does take part in an extended black face sequence which is best forgotten about by all involved. At best Biao's character at least gets some of the more genuine laughs from the loose narrative, and we do get a Biao versus Sammo rematch that's arguably the action highlight. However many of Don't Give a Damn's action scenes suffer from Sammo's mid-90's obsession with the step-printing technique (see also Thunderbolt and Ashes of Time), a fad we can be thankful fell out of fashion almost as fast as it came in. Overall though, seeing Biao and Sammo reunited onscreen again after 5 years leaves a strange aftertaste, and not necessarily a pleasant one.

Whereas Sammo Hung spent the rest of the decade taking a step back from action, instead choosing to partake in straight-up comedies and dramas, Biao continued travelling the rocky road as a kung fu leading man despite the genre losing popularity with local audiences. Later in the same year he'd headline the hilariously titled Tough Beauty and the Sloppy Slop. General consensus is that the 'Slop' is actually supposed to be 'Cop', although admittedly once you've read the title as is it's hard to imagine it being anything else. If Circus Kids was meant to be Biao's Drunken Master II, then Tough Beauty and the Sloppy Slop is clearly meant to be his Police Story III: Supercop. Playing

re-branded as Cynthia Luster!), and in 1995 they were joined by Donnie Yen (for Asian Cop: High Voltage), Cynthia Khan (who starred in Angel on Fire earlier in the year), and of course Yuen Biao. All ended up in the Philippines for different reasons – Yen had a falling out with his mentor Yuen Woo-Ping on the previous year's Wing Chun, which in the tightly knit Hong Kong film community saw local offers dry up. Khan was a stalwart of the Girls with Guns genre that by this point was on its last legs, and after failing to re-invent herself in new wave wuxia's like Zen of Sword, Philippines shot action cheapies seemed the only way to go.

As for Biao, after the double whammy of Circus Kids and Don't Give a Damn, it likely remained his best bet for continuing to work. As depressing as all this sounds, Tough Beauty and the Sloppy Slop proves to be a heap of fun, making it my fourth best Biao flick of the 90's. Directed by fellow Seven Little Fortunes

a Hong Kong cop teamed up with a Mainland police captain played by Cynthia Khan, together they must reluctantly team up to take down a drug ring being run out of Hong Kong, the Mainland, and the Philippines. The latter is where Tough Beauty and the Sloppy Slop takes place, a country that became known as the place were Hong Kong action stars go when they no longer have box office clout on local shores. The likes of Philip Ko Fei and Yukari Oshima were already ready regular fixtures in the Philippines (with the later

member Yuen Bun along with Alan Chui, also onboard is Yuen Wah (basically playing the same role as he did in Police Story III: Supercop), Billy Chow, and since it's the Philippines, we get omni-present local star Monsour Del Rosario. Featuring the usual Philippines combination of willing stuntmen taking hard hitting falls, endless amounts of gunfire aimed at an equally endless stream of lackeys, and plenty of fight action, as a cheap and cheerful action flick there's a lot to enjoy. As a bonus Biao gets a rematch against Billy Chow, 5 years

after License to Steal, this time paired with Cynthia Khan for a high impact 2 versus 1. One thing you can never accuse the Hong Kong film industry of in its heyday is being predictable, and far from remaining in the Philippines, Biao was back making movies in Hong Kong just a year later. 1996's The Hero of Swallow is a true oddity of the era, and was the last movie from director Siu Sang. Mainly known for helming swordplay and fantasy themed wuxia's in the 1960's, The Hero of Swallow both looks and feels like a movie from at least 20 years earlier, with Biao cast as a kind of Iron Monkey style character who robs from the rich and gives to the poor. A production that's the epitome of being out of time from the year it was made, Biao anchors proceedings surprisingly well as a character hunting for his lost love, played by Athena Chu who's been sold into a prostitution ring. There's an underlying charm and innocence to The Hero of Swallow that belies its obvious budgetary limitations, with Biao again adjusting his action style to a wirework infused performance courtesy of choreographer Lam Moon-Wa. Out of all the productions that Biao headlined during his career, even the really awful

ones, it's this one that feels like the forgotten gem in his filmography, and if approached with the right expectations (imagine Biao headlining a mid-70's Shaw Brothers flick!) there's plenty to enjoy. As was the case for most of Biao's filmography in the 90's though, for every couple of enjoyable entries, there was one unwatchable disaster. Joining the undesirable ranks alongside Saga of the Phoenix and Circus Kids, is 1996's Dragon in Shaolin. Neither a Hong Kong, Japanese, or Philippines shot production, this was the only time for Biao to appear in a Taiwanese movie, and it's in the form of the Taiwanese kids flick, a genre that's as distinct as it is dreaded. Sammo Hung had already subjected himself to making a genre appearance thanks to Chu Yen-Ping's 1993 cringe fest King Swindler, however even without Yen-Ping at the helm; Dragon in Shaolin is a special kind of insufferable. While it's minimum consolation, Biao at least isn't the main character, with the focus being on 2 kids – 1 a young monk and the other a street urchin. He enters the picture as an Indiana Jones styled adventurer who's journeying to return a buddha's head to a statue in China (ok, I'll say it again – if there was no Yuen Biao, there would be no Ong Bak!), and the pair of kids end up following him while being pursued by villainous art dealers. While gags involving kids peeing seemed to be an almost exclusive mainstay of 70's kung fu comedies, in Taiwan such jokes apparently never got old. Not only do we have to watch a kid peeing in Dragon in Shaolin, we also have to watch our main character tie a rock to his member as part of a street performance, and proceed to enthusiastically swing it around for the cheering audience. Call it cultural differences, but there's only so much of a kids crown jewels I can see in one movie (and by 'so much', I mean preferably none), and Dragon in Shaolin goes way over that limit. It's often brought up in discussions on Dragon in Shaolin that it could have been better if there was more of Biao, however I tend to disagree, and would say the less he's onscreen the better. The question at hand is how do you follow-up a movie which involves kids performing genitalia gymnastics? The answer, surprisingly, is probably Biao's most well-known role from the 90's, when he joined the cast of the Shaw Brothers comeback movie Hero in 1997. A remake of Shaw Brothers own Chang Cheh helmed classic The Boxer from Shantung, while Takeshi Kaneshiro takes on the iconic role of Ma Yung-Chen, it's Yuen Biao who clocks in a scene stealing performance as the gangster (played by David Chiang in the original) that takes Kaneshiro under his wing.

Reuniting Biao with Righting Wrongs director Corey Yuen for the first time in the roles of actor and director since the 1986 classic, it's a joy to see Biao taking on a prominent role in a lavishly budgeted production, the last of which was 1990's Shanghai Shanghai (which Corey Yuen was on choreography duty for). Biao's role in Hero could almost be viewed as the equivalent of Sammo Hung's role in Shanghai Shanghai, and seeing him

unleash his kicks decked out in a dapper suit while brandishing an axe is an undeniable pleasure. Hero is especially notable as it marks one of the last times to see 4 of the Seven Little Fortunes onscreen together, and still being able to perform a level of physically demanding action representative of what they could do in their prime. Corey Yuen also takes on choreography duties alongside Yuen Tak, who plays the villain of the piece, and Yuen Wah is on board for the ride as well.
In many ways Hero felt like Biao's return to the upper echelons of the Hong Kong action industry, one that saw him come back all guns blazing – both figuratively and literally, and for that reason I rank Hero as Biao's fifth best movie of the 90's. Of course for things to stay that way the timing also had to be right, and unfortunately Hero was released at a somewhat tumultuous time in the Hong Kong film industry. Released the year Hong Kong was handed back to the Mainland, many of the territories biggest names had already jumped ship to try their hand at Hollywood (Corey Yuen himself would leave to direct 2002's The Transporter), and kung fu flicks remained out of fashion despite a positive reception. The result saw the Shaw Brothers studio return to filmmaking quickly put back on pause, and they wouldn't try their hand again at a feature length production until Drunken Monkey 6 years later.
Frustratingly, while Hero hit Hong Kong cinemas in June, just 4 months later another Biao flick hit in the form of The Hunted Hunter, and just like that he was back in the Philippines shooting action cheapies. The Hunted Hunter doesn't just see Biao's return to the Philippines though, it's also the last legitimate time he can be considered the headlining star of a movie, with the next 25 years primarily consisting of TV work and supporting roles. While it would have been nice for Biao's last starring vehicle see him go out with a bang, unfortunately The Hunted Hunter clearly has even less of a budget behind it than his previous Philippines shot movie Tough Beauty and the Sloppy Slop. It does mark a reunion with director Ricky Lau, who previously worked with Biao as director on 1996's Mr Vampire Part 2 (it seems 1997 was the year for Biao to reunite with directors he'd worked with in 1986), and if anything it casts Biao in his grittiest role since 1988's On the Run.
Riffing on the The Fugitive, Biao plays a

security guard for a corporate building in which a murdered female office worker is discovered. As the only other person in the building at the time of death, Biao is convicted of the murder, and goes on the run to uncover the truth before he can be imprisoned. Yuen Bo's choreography goes for a hard-edged feel, with Biao at one point wielding a police baton in each hand which he isn't afraid to use during his escape attempt, and he also gets to let loose with a shot gun. However whereas Monsour Del Rosario fit in well in Tough Beauty and the Sloppy Slop, here local Filipino actors Roi Vinzon and Karen Timbol are insufferable as a pair of Manila cops on Biao's tail who eventually end up teaming up with him. Biao at least gets a worthy fight against Chung Fat, a rematch of their face off in 1985's Twinkle Twinkle Lucky Stars, and the final 15 minutes consist of the usual Philippines go-to action formula of plentiful gun fire again streams of regenerating lackeys. However for some of the earlier action scenes the dreaded step printing technique rears its head again, inexplicably robbing some of Biao's action scenes of any immediacy or sense of impact. Ironically Biao's last starring role also coincided with the Philippines itself losing its appeal as a location to shoot action cheapies, with the likes of Philip Ko Fei's Techno Warriors from the same year and 1998's Jade Leung vehicle Leopard Hunting being some of the last productions to film there. It was in 1998 that Biao stepped away from the big screen all together, and instead turned to TV work, returning to Taiwan to star in the 31-episode series The Righteous Guards, which reunited him with Cynthia Khan from Tough Beauty and the Sloppy Slop. It was also the first time for Biao to star alongside Shaw Brothers legend Ti Lung, and it proved to be enough of a fruitful experience that he clocked in a 2nd TV series during the same year, this time with the Mainland produced The Legend of a Chinese Hero, which consisted of 40 episodes. While it would be unfair to compare Biao's ventures on the small screen to his cinematic work, if anything at this point in his career it seemed that Biao himself was looking to wind down, and the less physically demanding TV roles were a good match for where he was at. He still fights plenty of times, but gone are the hard falls and stunt work, with more of a focus on story and drama. If it's surprising that Biao started the 90's by spending almost the entire runtime of a movie being frozen in a block of ice, then considering the ups and downs throughout the decade, it's perhaps even more surprising that he finished the 90's by returning to the big screen in a Golden Harvest production. A Man Called Hero was the middle entry in what's looked at as director Andrew Lau's CGI heavy marital arts trilogy that he closed out the 90's and started the new millennium with (the other 2 being 1998's Storm Riders and 2000's The Duel). In this case though, Biao takes on a supporting role, with the main star being Ekin Cheng. Biao's role in A Man Called Hero still allows him to flex his action chops as the righteous boss of the restaurant China House, and he spends his screen time decked out in a Chen Zhen styled white suit looking suitably cool, however it's clear he's no longer the star of the show.

So, with all evidence submitted and reviewed, what's the final verdict on Yuen Biao's 90's era – a complete whitewash, or are there some diamonds in the rough? I'll argue for the latter. Like stereotypes, broad brushstrokes usually also have some element of truth in them, and it's true that Biao's work during the decade frequently veered into the low budget combined with not being as physically dexterous as he once was. However those that choose to disregard the decade would be missing out on some legitimate entertainment. With my top 5 Biao flicks of the 90's summarised below – including wild new wave wuxia's, Philippines shot action cheapies, and studio comeback vehicles – there should be something for everyone!

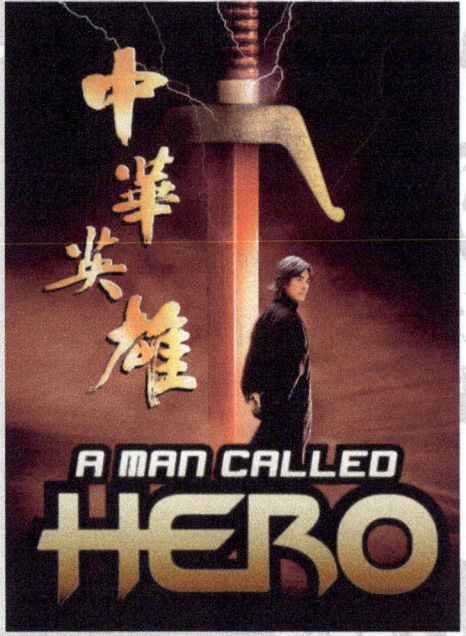

YUEN BIAO
LEADING MAN OF ACTION

"Rediscovering the Talents of Yuen Biao: A New Era of Appreciation for the Hong Kong Action Star"

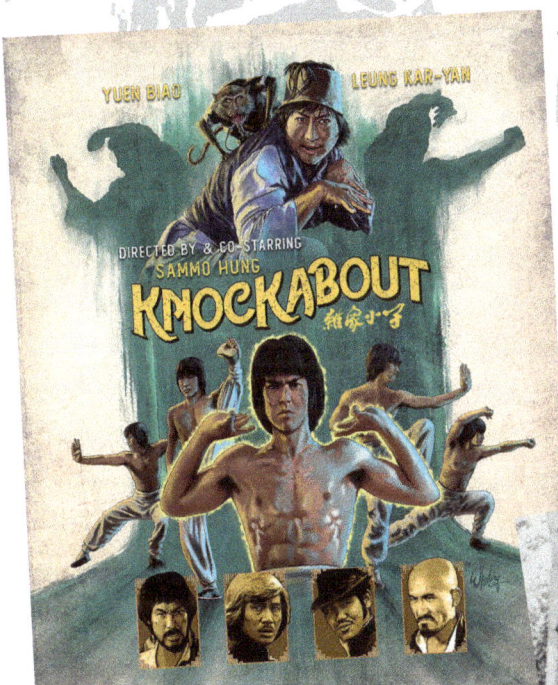

"Lucky Stars" trilogy, beginning with "Winners and Sinners" and ending with "Dragons Forever."

Thanks to new restorations being sold by boutique labels like the classic "Knockabout" and "Dreadnaught," Biao is now finally getting the recognition he deserves. "Knockabout" is a standout in Biao's early career, where he had primarily worked as a stuntman and extra. The film marked Biao's transition from co-star to

lead and embodies his comedic and athletic abilities. He starts as a double act with Liang Chia-jen, playing his brother and partner in crime, and demonstrates infectiously goofy on-screen chemistry. As the film progresses, Biao's acrobatic abilities take centre stage in a a fight scene that is both spectacular and silly. He starts as a double act with Liang Chia-jen, playing his brother and partner in crime, and demonstrates infectiously goofy on-screen chemistry. As the film progresses, Biao's acrobatic abilities take centre stage in a an extended showdown finale fight scene that is both spectacular and silly.

Yuen Biao is a name that deserves recognition in the world of Hong Kong action comedy. With his impressive athleticism, comedic timing, and acrobatics, Biao stands apart from his peers, Sammo Hung and Jackie Chan, who was also part of the Peking Opera School. Despite his considerable talent, Biao is often overlooked in discussions about the films of the Hong Kong martial arts scene, particularly in the Western world.

Biao's style of performance is both in sync with and distinct from that of Hung and Chan. He has the same expert comedic timing, a willingness to look foolish, combined with speed, flexibility, and a talent for dazzling acrobatics that sets him apart from both. This can be seen in his work with his Peking Opera brothers in the

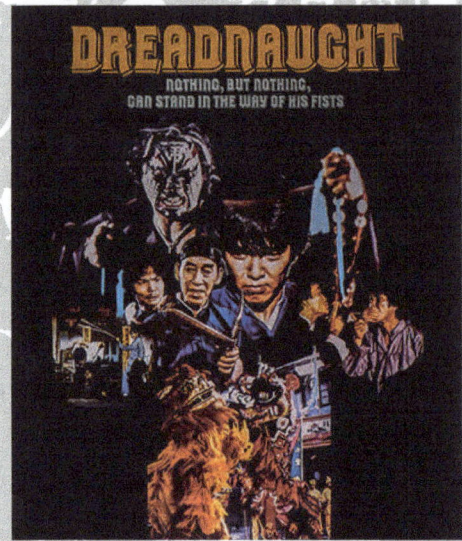

In "Dreadnaught," Biao takes on a completely different role as the hapless and clumsy outsider, Mousy. Despite his early career highlighting his athletic talents, Biao manages to convince the audience of his physical vulnerability while still remaining a convincing action lead. He manages to walk the tightrope of constantly showing physical vulnerability while still being a convincing action lead. In "Dreadnaught," Biao's victory comes not through physical strength but through the application of his "laundry kung fu." This film showcases Biao's range as an actor and his ability to play both authoritative figures and sweet-natured comic relief characters.

In conclusion, Yuen Biao's talent as a Hong Kong action star should not be underestimated. With his versatility, athleticism, and comedic timing, Biao is a force to be reckoned with in the world of Peking Opera and Hong Kong action films. It is time for the Western world to discover and appreciate the hidden talents of this exceptional performer.

元彪 Yuen Biao
KUNG FU KING
By Tim Hollingsworth

Just like me, a lot of people reading this may have discovered Yuen Biao via Jackie Chan. Back in the late 80's and early 90's Video shops were packed with jackie Chan titles, many of which also featured Sammo Hung and of course Yuen Biao himself. I always felt he was overshadowed by Jackie, Sammo in some repsct as well, due to the marketing of jackie being at the forefront. Having said that, Yuen Biao always caught my eye and soon became my go to Hong Kong action star. Back when I first started collecting Hong Kong movies, aside from Blockbuster Video, mail order was the go-to place for ordering films not available on the high street. I started trying to dig out anything Biao was in and also started noticing him in supporting roles and stunt work. With my love for martial arts films I started seeing Yuen Biao pop up in films as a henchman here and there. From the likes of secret Rivals starring John Liu, Invincible Armour, the Bruce Lee films, and an eagle eye will see him doubling for Tong Lung in The Game of Death 2. Anyway the list goes on and on but it was clear that Biao was a skilled stuntman, martial artist and gymnast which in most films never fails to throw in some flips, kicks and the odd crazy stunt here and there.

So, it's clear I like Yuen Biao and this issue of Eastern Heroes magazine is long ovedue in my eyes, so I've spent a while scanning various media i've collected over the years since the late 80's from VHS and DVD's, lobby cards, posters and images from various scources like magazines, articles and adverts etc. It's not everything I have but it's a start, So in no particular order... here we go!

KNOCKABOUT MEGASTAR VCD COVERS AND INSERTS

RED REVENGE

SPECIAL COLLECTOR'S EDITION

Featuring an all-star line-up of some of Hong Kong Cinema's most prolific action stars, 'Eastern Condors' is regarded by many enthusiasts as one of the crowning achievements of Sammo Hung's celebrated career.

In a powerful high-energy tribute to "The Dirty Dozen", ten soldiers condemned to life-term prison sentences are offered an amnesty if they go behind enemy lines in Vietnam to destroy a top-secret munitions dump.

DVD SPECIAL FEATURES

- Digitally re-mastered and restored DVD transfer
- 16:9 Anamorphic version enhanced for widescreen TVs
- Animated Biography Showcase
- Dual language format (English Dubbed and Cantonese Language with re-mastered English subtitles)
- AC3 5.1 Digital Audio
- Original Theatrical Trailer (including rare deleted footage)
- UK Promotional Trailer
- Interview Gallery with Sammo Hung

Action-legend Sammo Hung took preparations for this movie more seriously than any other, and hired personal trainer 'Eddie Mayer' to slim him down so he could more easily perform some of the incredible acrobatic kicking combinations which he had devised for the project with his stunt team.

Showcasing some of the most amazing fight and stunt sequences you will ever see, "Eastern Condors" is an awesome tribute to the physical genius of Sammo Hung. In a bid to capture a level of realism seldom seen on celluloid, most of the sequences in this movie were filmed for real, with the actors actually making full physical contact during the fight scenes.

Now restored and digitally re-mastered for it's UK premiere DVD release, and featuring a frank and revealing interview with director/star Sammo Hung on the making of the film, "Eastern Condors: Special Edition" is one of the most exciting, raw-edged DVD packages you will ever experience!!

Starring: Sammo Hung, Yuen Biao, Joyce Godenzi
Directed by: Sammo Hung   Produced by: Leonard K.C. Ho   Action by: Sammo Hung

HONG KONG LEGENDS

SAMMO HUNG
YUEN BIAO
JOYCE GODENZI

EASTERN CONDORS

DIGITALLY RESTORED AND REMASTERED

The incomparable SAMMO HUNG (MILLIONAIRES' EXPRESS, HEART OF DRAGON and Jackie Chan's Mr. NICE GUY) directs and stars in this spectacular Vietnam War action epic, critically acclaimed by many as Hung's finest work. Three years after the Vietnam War ends, a group of Chinese convicts are recruited by the U.S. Army to return to Vietnam. Their mission - to destroy a missile ammunition dump left behind by the Marines before it falls into the Vietcong's hands. With the vicious enemy in hot pursuit, this bunch of misfits must rely on their firepower - and themselves - to accomplish their mission, and to get out of the treacherous jungle alive.

With wall - to - wall gunfire action and an all - star cast that includes acrobatics sensation Yuen Biao, martial arts legend Yuen Woo Ping, and THE KILLING FIELDS' Dr. Haing S. Ngor, Sammo Hung's tough, gritty version of THE DIRTY DOZEN also features some of the most extraordinary fight sequences ever filmed. EASTERN CONDORS is a soaring masterpiece in the history of modern martial arts action cinema.

a SAMMO HUNG film "EASTERN CONDORS"
starring SAMMO HUNG / YUEN BIAO / NG HON directed by SAMMO HUNG
executive producer RAYMOND CHOW produced by LEONARD HO chief production manager CHAN PUI WAH
production manager AMY CHIN associate producer WU MA / RICKY LAU / COREY YUEN screenplay by BARRY WONG
action choreographer HUNG BROTHERS director of cinematography ARTHUR WONG art director LI KING MAN
edited by CHANG YAO CHUNG music by CHOW MING CHEUNG

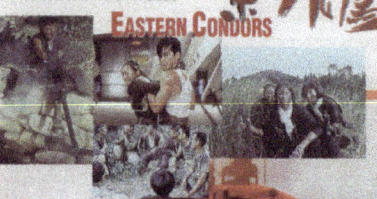

EASTERN CONDORS

directed by
Sammo Hung
starring **Sammo Hung   Yuen Biao**
produced by **LEONARD HO**

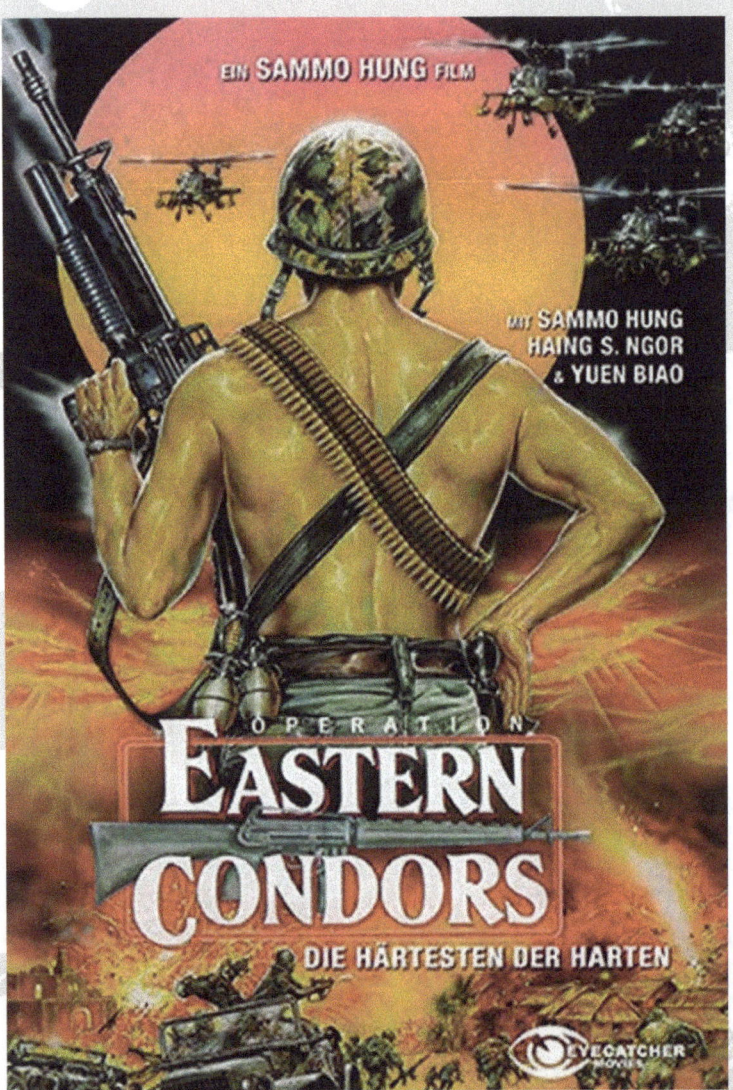

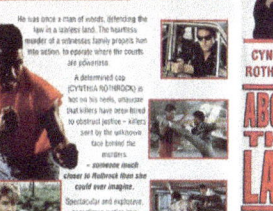

YUEN BIAO TAKES ON JACKIE CHAN IN THE YOUNG MASTER

YUEN BIAO
武術指導●ユン・ピョウ

ユン・ピョウ（元彪）——1957年7月26日、香港の九龍生まれ。兄1人、姉3人、妹3人の8人兄弟。6歳の時、ジャッキーやサモ・ハンを育てた中国戯劇学院に入り、みっちりしごかれる。17歳で学院を出ると、兄弟子のサモ・ハンが武術指導助手を勤める映画スタジオに出入りし、サモの助言で難しいアクションのスタントや、エキストラとして使われるようになった。

やがてクンフー映画の下火から、アメリカに渡ってクンフー・ショーなどに出演していたが食いつめ、再びサモの引きで香港へ。初めはサモの武術指導監督の助手をしていたが、サモのすすめで「猿拳」の主役をやったところこれが大ヒット。その後の作品は日本未公開が多いが、「プロジェクトA」で香港はもとより日本でも人気者となった。サモやジャッキーが弟のようにかわいがり、「スパルタンX」「五福星」「大福星」などでトリオとして出演している。

私生活ではサモの監督・出演作「ピックポケット」で武術指導した時に知りあった女優のディディー・パンと1982年4月に結婚している。

主な出演作品 ⑦燃えよドラゴン ⑱死亡遊戯 ⑲猿拳 ⑳ヤングマスター ㉞プロジェクトA、五福星、スパルタンX ㉟チャンピオン鷹、大福星

主演 ユン・ピョウ ジョイス・コウ

元彪

元彪

元彪

EYEING UP THE CLOCKTOWER IN PROJECT A

RED REVENGE

一代英雄—鬼腳七
揚名立萬英勇事蹟
勁拳頭 酷腳法 真功夫

黃飛鴻之鬼腳七

本片描述敗家仔到七（元彪飾演）為父所逼，入寶芝林拜師學藝，揚名立萬，被推崇為「鬼腳七」的一段故事。

年少時的鬼腳七好打不平，為救女記者小霎（呂秀菱飾演），出手擊退洋人，但誤交損友，被利用偷運鴉片，逼連累師兄牙擦蘇（午馬飾演），七無故受屈，遣人唾棄，且被廣州府禁毒老羞骨山東役（任世官飾演），諸多留難。時值黃師傅往南洋未返，寶芝林內無人主持公道，只有胡細珍（陳淑蘭飾演）因心疼七，從中安撫。

While master Wong Fei Hung is away traveling, the impulsive Lau Zhai (Yuen Biao), an initiate into Wong's kung fu school, begins wandering town. He soon allies with police chief Panther in order to offer assistance in toppling an opium distribution ring.

導演：午馬　　劇本：李敏才
演員：元彪 午馬 元華 陳湘蘭 太保 任世官 元奎 呂琇菱 Yukan Tamura 任細官 常山 金十二
製作人：元彪一監製　　繆騰江一製片
攝影：黃仲標　副導演助理導演：趙籠江 林克明
Golden Tripod Film Co., HK   Yuen Biao Films Co., Ltd.

KICK BOXER

黃飛鴻之
動作／武術指導／演出
鬼腳七
元彪

KICK BOXER

Once upon a time in China 6
KICKBOXER

鬼腳七

Hong Kong superstar Yuen Biao stars as "Clubfoot" in this brilliant chapter in the Wong Fei Hung (Once Upon a Time in China) saga. The Master of Chess has teamed up with the Eagle Claw King and have started trading in Opium with the British. Only Clubfoot stands against them.

ENGLISH VERSION .   **WIDE SCREEN .**
YUEN BIAO SPECIAL .   **89 MINS .**

ALL RIGHTS RESERVED YUEN BIAO FILMS (HK)   DVD.COM.LTD   DC0078

AKA: Once upon a Chinese hero

Starring: Yuen Biao, Yuen Hwa, Chang Shan, Yen Shi Kwan
Produced by: Yuen Biao   Action Director: Yuen Biao, Yuen Mao

VENGEANCE VIDEO

RED REVENGE

Visit our website at: http://www.hongkonglegends.com
For independent Hong Kong Legends reviews and much more visit http://www.bbc.co.uk/films

If you would like to comment on any of our titles, or require further information or details of future releases, please contact us at:
Hong Kong Legends, PO Box 88, Hitchin SG5 1FL, United Kingdom.
E-mail: enquiries@hongkonglegends.co.uk

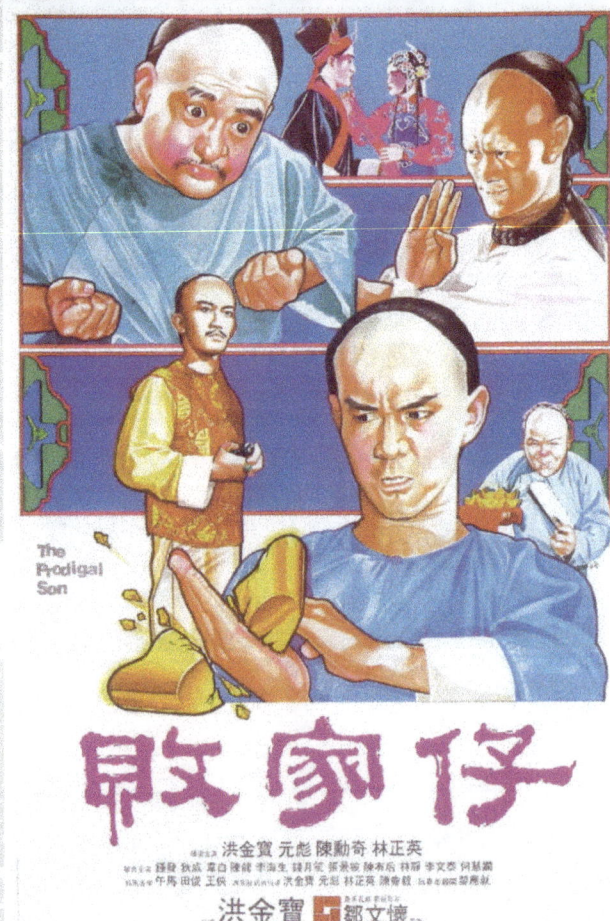

DREADNAUGHT
aka Prodigal Son 2
FROM YUEN WOO PING
THE ACTION DIRECTOR
OF THE MATRIX TRILOGY
AND KILL BILL 1 & 2

勇者無懼

YUEN BIAO
DREAD
NAUGHT

YUEN BIAO
LEUNG KAR-YAN
DIRECTED BY YUEN WOO-PING
DREADNAUGHT

LEGENDARY
勇者無懼

勇者無懼
DVD
yesasia.com

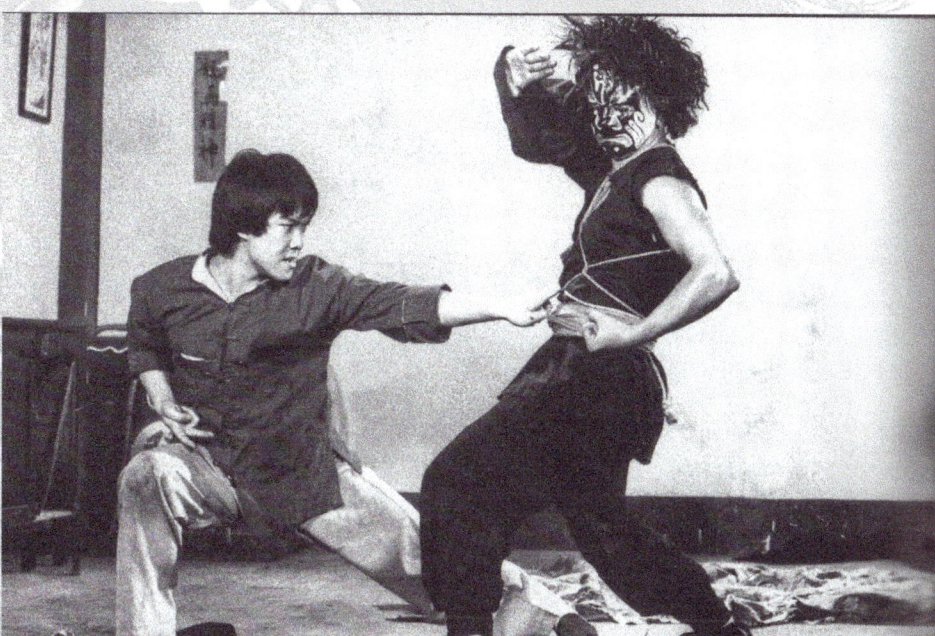

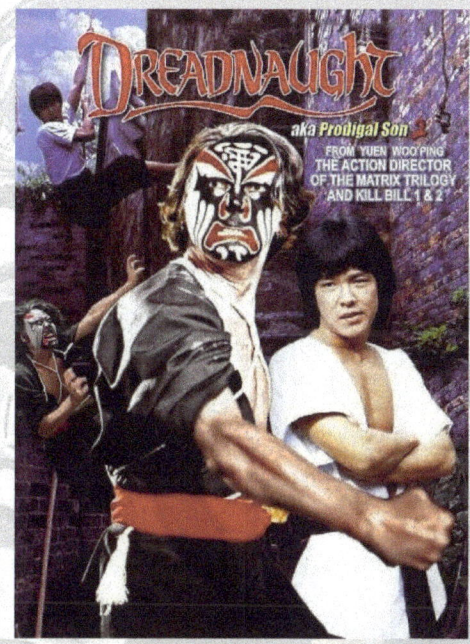

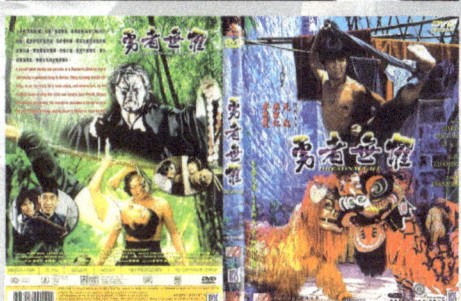

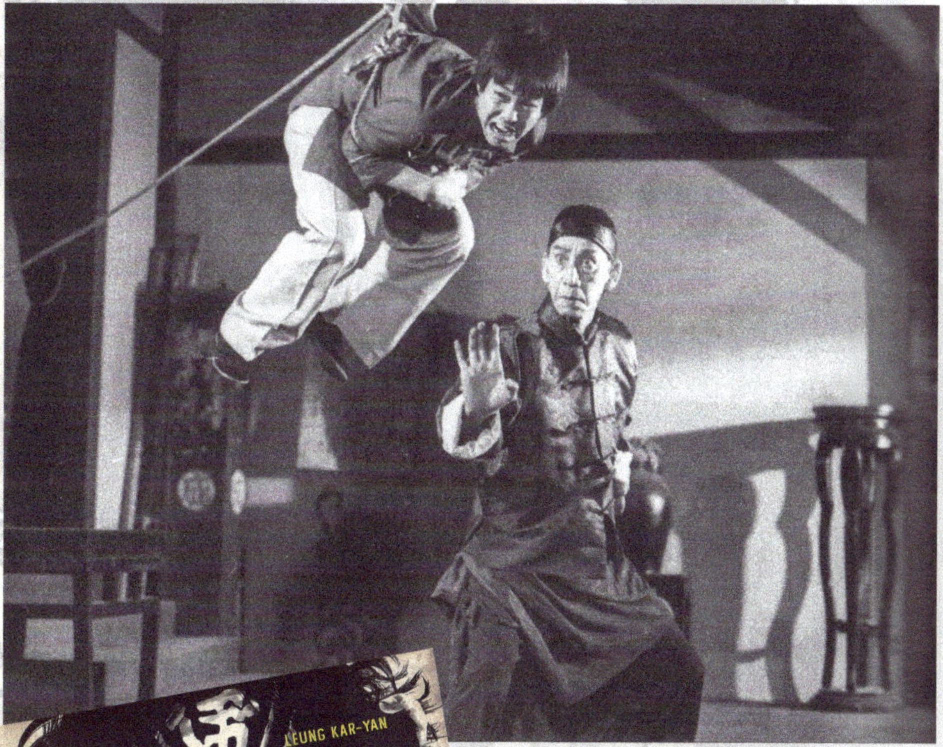

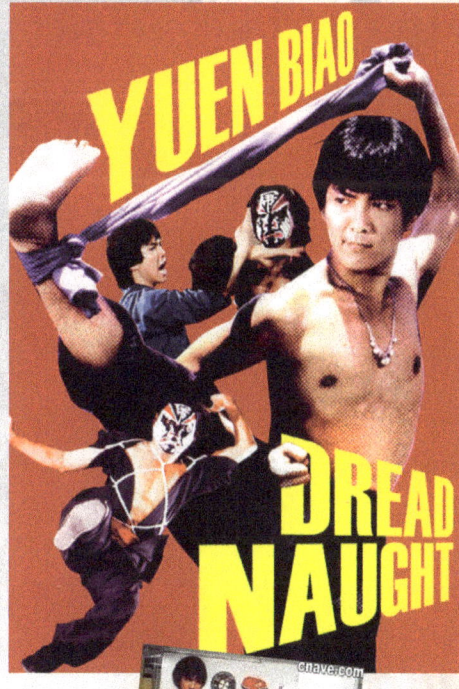

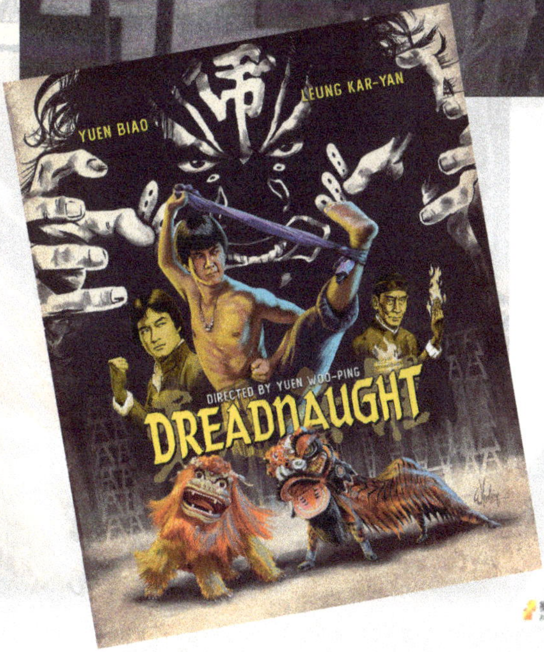

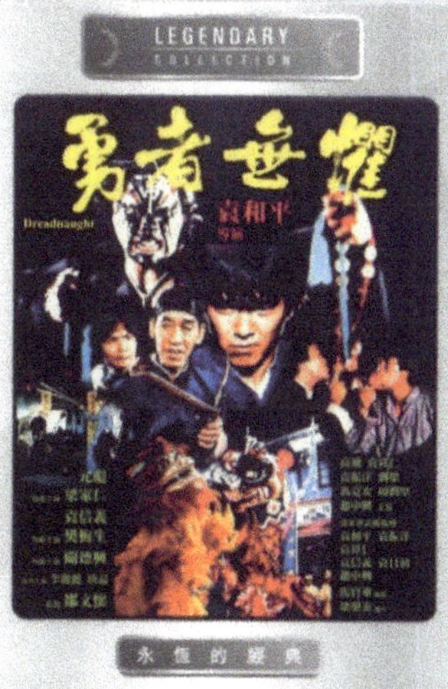

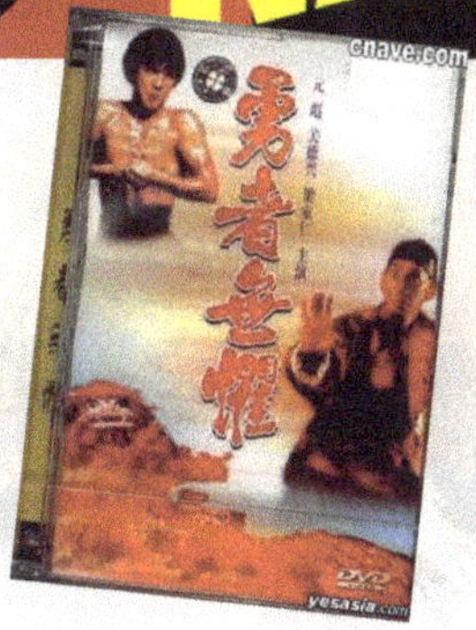

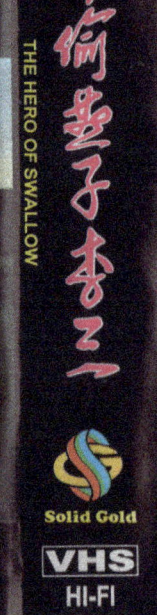

the 3 LEGENDS of Hong Hong Cinema
An overview By Rick Baker
Sammo Hung, Jackie Chan & Yuen Biao

The world of cinema is filled with numerous names, but few can match the fame and respect that Sammo Hung, Jackie Chan, and Yuen Biao have earned. These three legends of Hong Kong cinema are well-known for their martial arts skills, acting prowess, and directing abilities. They made their mark in the late 70s into the 1980s, during the golden age of Hong Kong cinema, where they emerged as some of the most iconic action stars in film history.

Their story began at the Peking Opera School, which was also known as the China Drama Academy. It was a training ground for young actors and martial artists in Hong Kong. The Three Dragons, as we affectionately refer to, honed their skills in martial arts, acrobatics, and acting here. They trained together for years, mastering the traditional techniques of Peking Opera and developing their own unique styles in the process.

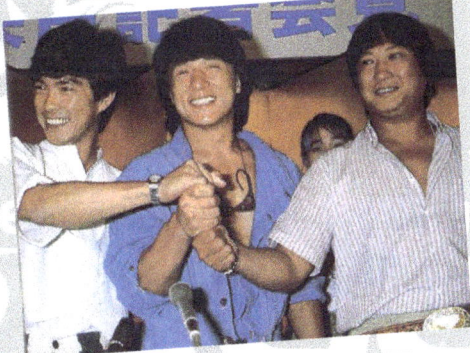

Their first big splash in the film industry was in the 1970s when they appeared in a number of kung Fu as extras progressing to leading roles in movies that showcased their incredible martial arts skills. They quickly became popular with audiences and soon found themselves in high demand, appearing in film after film and establishing themselves as some of the most talented and exciting new stars in the industry.

In the 1980s, the Three Dragons joined forces with the Hong Kong film studio Golden Harvest, which was at the forefront of the Hong Kong New Wave. It was here that they made some of their most memorable and successful films,

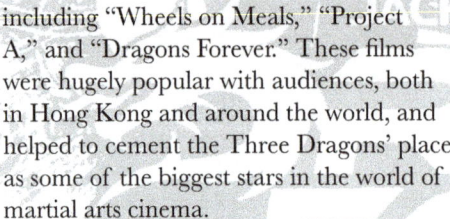

including "Wheels on Meals," "Project A," and "Dragons Forever." These films were hugely popular with audiences, both in Hong Kong and around the world, and helped to cement the Three Dragons' place as some of the biggest stars in the world of martial arts cinema.

Their films were more than just action-packed; they also brought a sense of humour and light-heartedness to the genre, which had previously been dominated by more serious and stylized martial arts films. This approach helped to make their films more accessible and appealing to a wider audience, and helped to establish them as the leading figures in the world of Hong Kong action cinema.

Sammo Hung, Jackie Chan, and Yuen Biao have left an indelible mark on the world of martial arts cinema. Their innovative and entertaining films continue to be popular

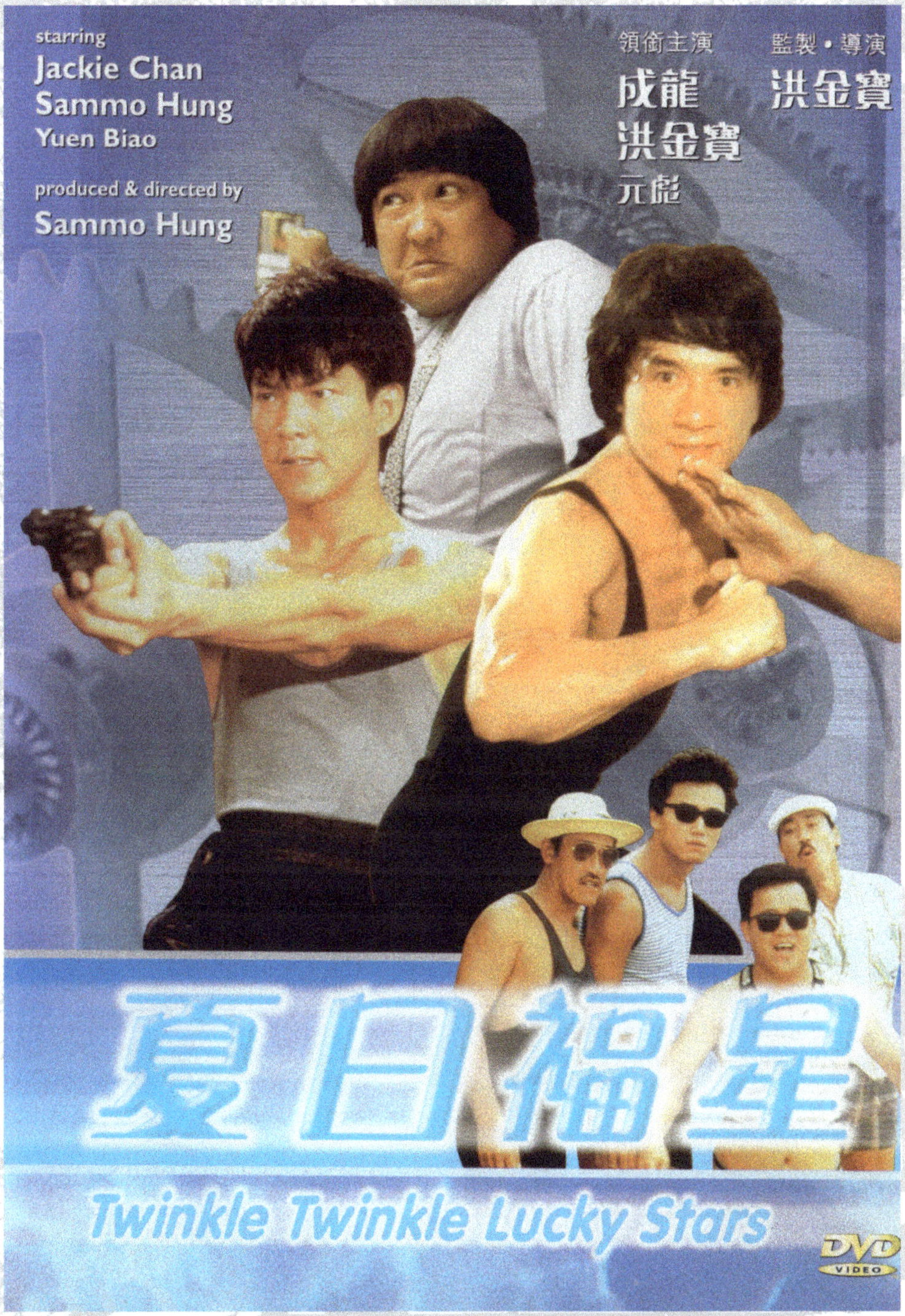
starring
Jackie Chan
Sammo Hung
Yuen Biao
produced & directed by
Sammo Hung
領銜主演
成龍
洪金寶
元彪
監製・導演
洪金寶
夏日福星
Twinkle Twinkle Lucky Stars
DVD
VIDEO

FORTUNE STAR
福星高照
dts
DVD

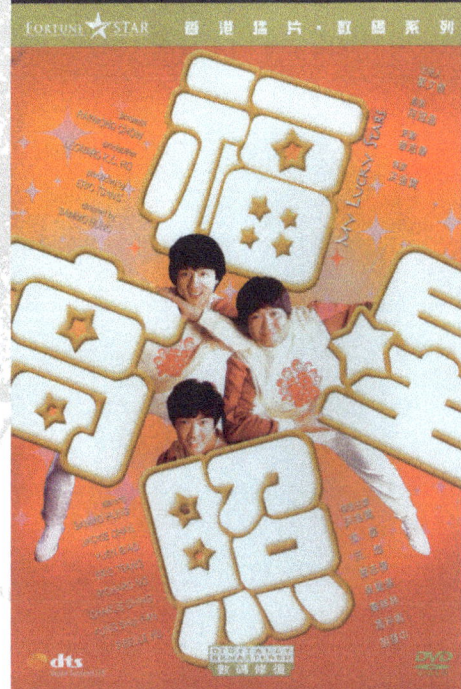

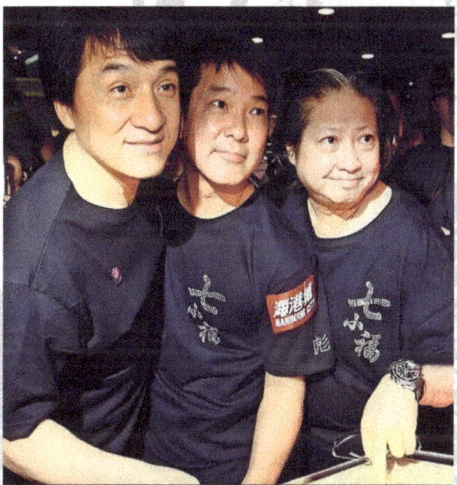

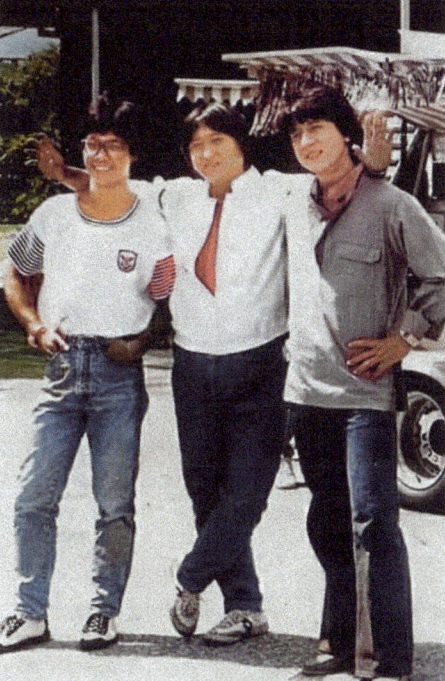

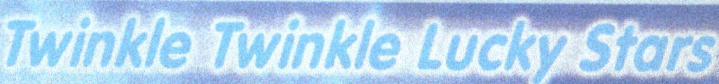

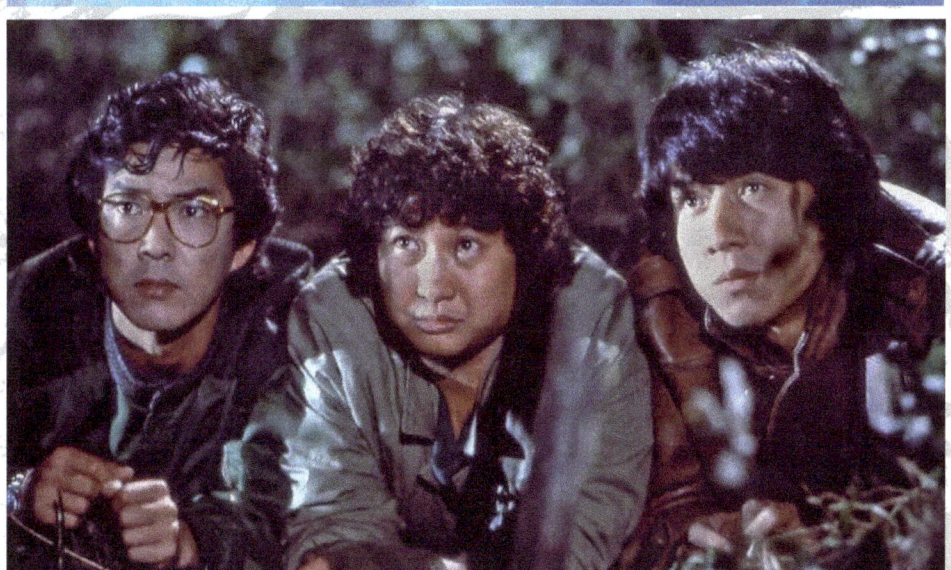

with audiences around the world, and their status as some of the greatest martial artists and action stars of all time is secure. They are remembered as legends of the Hong Kong film industry, and their impact on the world of cinema is still felt.

Aside from their contributions to Hong Kong cinema, the Three Dragons also have a significant influence on the global film industry. Jackie Chan, for instance, is known for his unique blend of comedy and action, which has become a trademark in his films. He has appeared in numerous Hollywood movies, such as "Rush Hour," "Shanghai Noon," and "The Karate Kid," where he introduced his brand of martial arts to international audiences. Sammo Hung, on the other hand, is known for his unique style of action choreography, which combines comedy, drama, and traditional martial arts techniques. He has worked with Hollywood actors and directors including his breakthrough series "Martial Law". Yuen Biao has not had the same success as his two brothers in arms overseas.

In conclusion, the Three Dragons of Hong Kong cinema - Sammo Hung, Jackie Chan, and Yuen Biao - are true legends of the film industry. Their mastery of martial arts, acting, and directing has left an indelible mark on the world of cinema, and their films continue to captivate audiences around the world. But sadly due to age and in the case of Sammo Hung ill health it is very unlikely that we will get are fan wish to see them once again perform together. But to us there impact will live on as we say here in the west "Dragons are forever"

FUN FACTS ABOUT YUEN BIAO

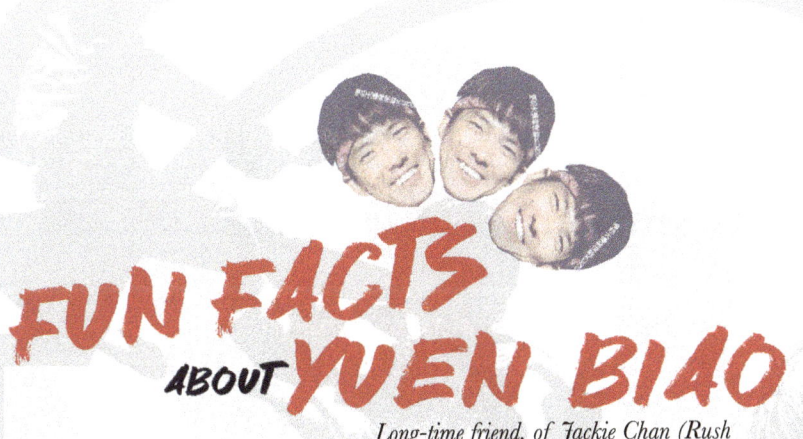

Long-time friend, of Jackie Chan (Rush Hour (1998)) and Sammo Kam-Bo Hung (Martial Law (1998)

Attended Peking Opera school, run by Jim-Yuen Yu who moved to Hong Kong from Mainland China. By the time Yuen Biao, Jackie Chan, and Sammo Kam-Bo Hung graduated, Peking Opera performances were declining in popularity (a fictionalized account is told in Painted Faces 1988, starring Sammo Hung as their infamously strict teacher Yu Jim Yuen.) These graduates skilled in Peking Opera and martial arts then entered film business to apply their life-long skills, transforming the waning swordplay and (old school) kung fu genres in 1970s-1980s, and inventing the now classic, multi-genre modern action of 1980s.

"Yuen" is the surname of his Peking Opera school teacher, Jim-Yuen Yu. Many school graduates take the name as their stage name, in honor of their teacher. "Biao" means a youthful tiger in its prime.

Introduced nephew Yuen-Man Fung to film production. Fung has now directed Futago (2005).

Is one of the rare HK performers who have a more loyal following in Japan than in his native Hong Kong. Thus the many Japan/HK co-productions in his work (The Setting Sun (1992), Baka yarô! 4 You! Omae no koto da yo 3 Sagi naru Japan (1991), No Problem 2 (2002).) For the Kung Fu-soccer comedy The Champions (1983)), he was promoted as a wholesome, super-athlete version of Japan's pop idol culture. As the norm for idols in Japan, Yuen released several music albums despite his rudimentary grasp on Japanese and pop music. Documented as recently as 2004, Yuen still makes the occasional personalized replies to his Japanese fans. Yuen Biao did not portray The Pickpocket, aka Little Frog, in Snake Fist Fighter (1973) (Snake Fist Fighter). The role was actually played by Kwok-Choi Hon.

He is one of the few to retain the "Yuen" name that he was forced to take on whilst a member of Yu Jim-Yuen's Chinese Drama Academy. Most of the other performers who studied at the same school - including Jackie Chan and Sammo Hung - stopped using their given "Yuen" names after leaving the Academy.

Yuen Biao was mistaken by some to be the brother of Korean martial arts director/action star Won Jin, due to their acrobatic skill and similar names, as Won Jin was translated to Yuen Jan in Cantonese.

Yuen Biao was the original action director for the movie Operation Scorpio (1992), but this role was ultimately performed by fellow "7 Little Fortunes" member Yuen Tak.

Biao has worn spectacles since adolescence. Although in most movies he does not not wear spectacles he can be seen wearing his own pairs in Wheels on Meals (1984), Mr. Vampire II (1986), and The Hunted Hunter (1997).

YUEN BIAO
THE SEVEN LITTLE FORTUNES

By Simon Pritchard

Yuen Biao is a Hong Kong actor, martial artist, and stuntman with over 130 films to his credit, Biao is considered one of the top stars in Hong Kong cinema.

Yuen Biao aka Ha Ling Chun (夏令震) was born on 26th July 1957 in British Hong Kong at home in Castle Peak Road. Biao was the fifth child in a middle class Chinese family of eight children. His parents, Ha Kwong-Tai and Ha Sau-Ying, were heavily influenced by the heritage of Kung Fu and at five years of age, (some say six), Biao was enrolled in the Peking Opera School – The China Drama Academy. It was ran from a small theatre in the Lai Chi Kok amusement park by Master Yu Jim-Yuen who passed away in 1997 at the age of 92. Master Yu Jim-Yuen named all his students under his family name "Yuen". Ha Ling Chun was given the stage name Yuen Biao (Little Tiger). Some of the actors continued to perform under his name and others took stage names. Some of the most notable students are:

Yuen Lo (Jackie Chan)
Yuen Long (Sammo Hung)
Yuen Biao
Corey Yuen
Yuen Wah
Yuen Qui
Yuen Tai

Master Yu was known as strict teacher and pushed his students hard. There are rumours that some students died during training but this is unsubstantiated. The best students were known as the Seven Little Fortunes which toured locally and internationally. It is said that more than seven students toured but only seven would perform at each show. The school also sent some students to work as extras in films to bring additional income into the school. Biao showed a lot of talent for kung fu and acrobatics at a young age with his 'cat' like movements. As a teenager Biao was considered better than his seniors. According to Jackie Chan's autobiography, Biao was one of the fastest to learn and when asked by his master to do a backflip on his first day of training, he did a backflip on his first try.

Biao remained at the school until the age of 16, where he moved with Master Yu to America. However, two years later he came back as he didn't think there were any roles for Chinese martial arts there. Upon return Biao worked with his old Peking Opera School brothers and their relationship has lasted for their entire careers. Biao was also portrayed as a child and as a teenager in Sammo's Painted Faces (1988) which is a biographical drama film, based on his time at the Peking Opera School. Biao commented that Painted Faces "offers a different take on their lives under Master Yu". Biao continued to work throughout his career behind the camera and performing stunts to try and step outside of Jackie and Sammo's shadow to prove he can succeed on his own.

Biao began work as a stuntman and extra in the early 1970's. After working on Fist of Fury and The Way of the Dragon, Biao progressed and became a stunt double for Bruce Lee on Enter the Dragon. Biao was also one of the 'fake' Bruce Lees in Game of Death performing the acrobatics and stunts that Bruce Lee's body-double, Taekwondo expert Kim Tai Chung, was unable to perform. During this time, Biao was given the anglicised name Bill Yuen for use on the Hong Kong films that were released internationally. However, recognising the growing success of Jackie Chan, Golden Harvest was keen to give him a similar name, and on some international film prints, he was credited as Jimmy Yuen which neither lasted long. Biao's stuntman and supporting roles were in some of the biggest kung fu films of that time including, Hapkido, Stoner, The Himalayan, Hand of Death, Shaolin Wooden Men, Broken Oath, Warriors Two, Enter the Fat Dragon, Spiritual Kung Fu, Magnificent Butcher. After co-starring in The Dragon, the Odds, Biao's first full lead role was Knockabout (1979). Biao then went on to star in several films notably The Prodigal Son, Dreadnaught.

Project A, Wheels on Meals and Dragons Forever with Jackie and Sammo, Righting Wrongs with Cynthia Rothrock, and The Iceman Cometh with Maggie Cheung. Biao also appeared in smaller roles in films such as Sammo's Lucky Stars trilogy, Encounters of the Spooky Kind, The Victim, The Avenging Fist, Rob-B-Hood, Turning Point, The Legend Is Born – Ip Man.

Biao made films up until 2014 and has only done a couple of Chinese TV cameos since. He has said the right scripts haven't been coming through. We hope the scripts come through and it would be amazing to see Biao back on the big screen.

PHOTO GALLERY

EASTERN CONDORS

"Eastern Condors," directed by the talented Sammo Hung and released in 1987, boasts an all-star cast, including Yuen Biao, Joyce Godenzi, Yuen Wah, Lam Ching-ying, Yuen Woo-ping, Corey Yuen, and Billy Chow. The film follows a group of Chinese American convicts who are sent on a dangerous mission to Vietnam to destroy an old American bunker filled with missiles in exchange for a pardon, U.S. citizenship, and $200,000 each.

Hung, who also stars in the lead role, was at his best weight for this movie, thanks to his rigorous training by Eddie Maher, who unfortunately is no longer with us. In order to keep him on a strict diet, they had to put a chain and padlock around the fridge. The film takes viewers on a thrilling journey through enemy territory, as the group faces numerous challenges and obstacles, including a POW camp where they are forced to play Russian roulette. As the story progresses, the group faces a traitor within their ranks and must fight off the Vietnamese military to reach the bunker and destroy the missiles.

The film features outstanding performances by the cast, with Hung leading the charge. The action sequences are expertly choreographed and executed, making for an incredibly exciting viewing experience.

Overall, "Eastern Condors" is a must-see for fans of action films and is a testament to Sammo Hung's skills as a director and actor. It's no wonder that it inspired the name of my magazine "Eastern Heroes", as it remains in my top five films to this day.

東方鷹鷹
EASTERN CONDORS

Page 55　Yuen Biao Special

Page 56 Yuen Biao Special

敗家仔

The Prodigal Son　監製 鄒文懷　嘉禾貢獻 最佳影片　編導 洪金寶　詠春拳顧問 黎應就　洪家班武術指導 林正英 洪金寶 元彪 陳會毅　特別客串 王俠 午馬 田俊　何慧嫻 林靜 李文泰 張景坡 陳有后 李海生 錢月笙　聯合主演 鍾發 狄威 韋白 陳龍　領銜主演 洪金寶 元彪 陳勳奇 林正英

The Prodigal Son
Directed by Sammo Hung
Starring Sammo Hung Yuen Biao Lam Ching-ying Frankie Chan

The Prodigal Son is a martial arts comedy film from 1981 that boasts an impressive cast of Yuen Biao and Sammo Hung, as well as outstanding performances from Lam Ching Ying and Frankie Chan. The film tells the story of Leung Chang, a wealthy man's son who is forced to pay people to lose to him in fights due to his lack of martial arts expertise.

Yuen Biao, who plays the lead role of Leung Chang, delivers a fantastic performance that is both comedic and action-packed. He seamlessly blends his comic timing with his martial arts skills, making for an entertaining and engaging performance. Sammo Hung, who plays a kung fu expert that Leung Chang tries to convince to take him on as a student, also delivers a solid performance and serves as a great foil to Biao's character.

However, Lam Ching Ying and Frankie Chan also put in some scene stealing performances that showcases their outstanding talent. Lam Ching Ying, who plays the role of Leung Chang's loyal servant, delivers a memorable and impactful performance that is both humorous and heart-warming. Frankie Chan, who plays one of the film's villains, also delivers a standout performance that showcases his impressive martial arts skills.

The fight scenes in The Prodigal Son are expertly choreographed and executed with precision, making for an intense and exciting viewing experience. The Wing Chun moves are especially impressive and are executed flawlessly by the cast. The film's success in this area is reflected by the fact

that it earned Hung, Biao and Lam Ching-ying Best Action Choreography honours at the 1983 Hong Kong Film Awards.

The impact that The Prodigal Son had on the martial arts movie world cannot be overstated. The film set a new standard for martial arts comedy films and inspired many imitators in the years that followed. Its success helped to establish Yuen Biao and Sammo Hung as major stars in the genre, and it remains a beloved and influential film It's impact on the martial arts movie world is still felt to this day, making it a true classic of the genre.

"Twinkle, Twinkle, Lucky Stars" is a 1985 Hong Kong action-comedy film that boasts an impressive cast, with the likes of Sammo Hung, Jackie Chan, and Yuen Biao in leading roles. Directed by Hung himself, the movie is a sequel to "Lucky Stars Go Places" and "Winners and Sinners."

The film follows three bumbling detectives who are tasked with stopping a group of international terrorists who are planning to steal a valuable ancient artifact. Sammo Hung stars as the lead detective, Muscles, who is known for his strength but not his brains. Jackie Chan plays Kidstuff, a cop who is not above using unorthodox methods to get the job done, while Yuen Biao takes on the role of the nimble and quick-witted Fastbuck.

The chemistry between the three lead actors is a highlight of the film, and their comedic timing is impeccable. The trio delivers some of the most entertaining action sequences in Hong Kong cinema history, with Hung's larger-than-life fighting style, Chan's acrobatic skills, and Biao's impressive martial arts prowess.

One of the most memorable scenes in the movie is the opening sequence, which features a high-speed chase on foot through the streets of Hong Kong. The scene sets the tone for the rest of the film, as it showcases the physical prowess of the lead actors and the humor that permeates throughout the entire movie.

Another notable scene is the climactic battle in which the three detectives take on the terrorists in a classic Hong Kong-style fight sequence. The fight choreography is well-executed, and the use of practical effects adds to the realism of the action.

Overall, "Twinkle, Twinkle, Lucky Stars" is an entertaining and action-packed movie that showcases the talents of its lead actors. It is a must-see for fans of Hong Kong cinema, as it perfectly encapsulates the style and energy of the genre.

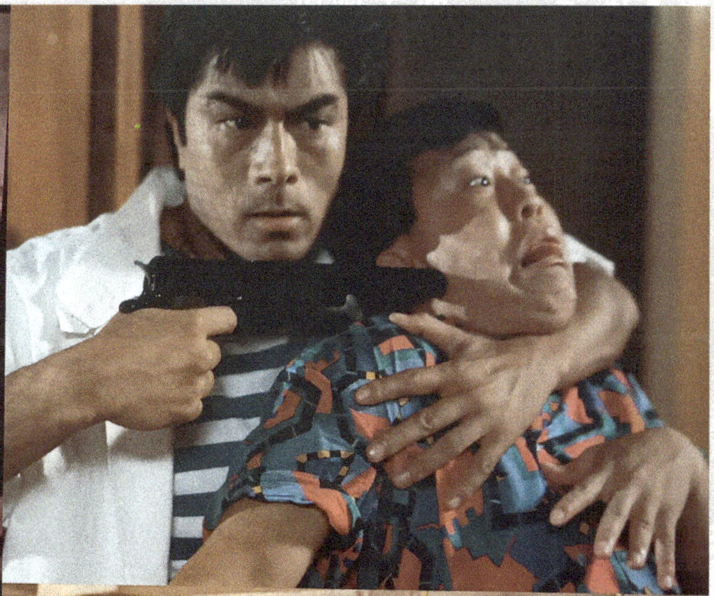

Page 65 Yuen Biao Special

WHEELS ON MEALS

Wheels on Meals" is a 1984 action-comedy film directed by Sammo Hung, who also stars in the film alongside Jackie Chan and Yuen Biao. The film tells the story of two best friends, Thomas (Chan) and David (Biao), who operate a mobile food truck in Barcelona, Spain, and find themselves caught up in a dangerous adventure when they meet a beautiful pickpocket named Sylvia (Lola Forner) and try to help her find her long-lost father. One of the strengths of "Wheels on Meals" is the dynamic chemistry between the three main characters. Jackie Chan plays Thomas, a kung-fu expert and ladies' man who is always ready for a fight. Yuen Biao plays David, a more reserved and thoughtful character who is also highly skilled in martial arts. Sammo Hung plays Moby, a bumbling private investigator who is constantly trying to track down Sylvia's father. The interactions between these three characters are a joy to watch, as they each bring their own unique personality and fighting style to the mix. Jackie Chan's trademark acrobatic fighting moves are on full display, while Yuen Biao's graceful athleticism is equally impressive. Sammo Hung's character provides comic relief and adds an extra layer of chaos to the already frenetic action scenes.

Aside from the dynamic between the main characters, "Wheels on Meals" also stands out for its stunning location and excellent choreography. The film is set in Barcelona, Spain, and takes full advantage of the city's vibrant energy and iconic landmarks. The action scenes are expertly choreographed, with a mix of traditional kung-fu moves and creative stunts that showcase the talents of the three leads.

Overall, "Wheels on Meals" is a highly entertaining action-comedy that showcases the talents of Jackie Chan, Yuen Biao, and Sammo Hung. The film is a must-see for fans of martial arts movies and anyone who appreciates a good old-fashioned buddy comedy. With its thrilling action scenes, comedic moments, and charismatic performances, "Wheels on Meals" is a classic of the genre that still holds up today.

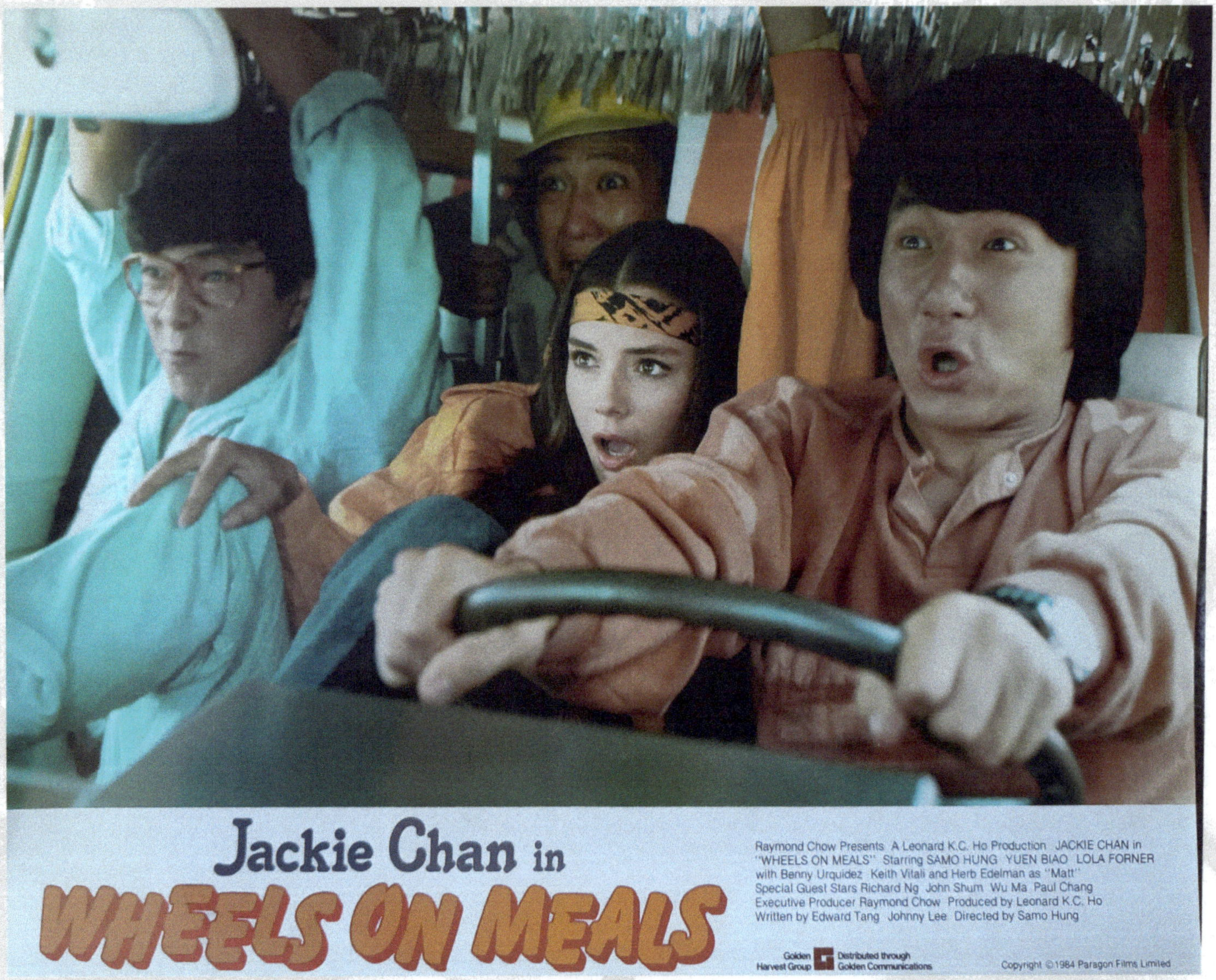
Jackie Chan in
WHEELS ON MEALS
Raymond Chow Presents A Leonard K.C. Ho Production JACKIE CHAN in
"WHEELS ON MEALS" Starring SAMO HUNG YUEN BIAO LOLA FORNER
with Benny Urquidez Keith Vitali and Herb Edelman as "Matt"
Special Guest Stars Richard Ng John Shum Wu Ma Paul Chang
Executive Producer Raymond Chow Produced by Leonard K.C. Ho
Written by Edward Tang Johnny Lee Directed by Samo Hung
Golden Harvest Group
Distributed through Golden Communications
Copyright ©1984 Paragon Films Limited

Jackie Chan in
WHEELS ON MEALS
Raymond Chow Presents A Leonard K.C. Ho Production JACKIE CHAN in
"WHEELS ON MEALS" Starring SAMO HUNG YUEN BIAO LOLA FORNER
with Benny Urquidez Keith Vitali and Herb Edelman as "Matt"
Special Guest Stars Richard Ng John Shum Wu Ma Paul Chang
Executive Producer Raymond Chow Produced by Leonard K.C. Ho
Written by Edward Tang Johnny Lee Directed by Samo Hung
Golden Harvest Group
Distributed through Golden Communications

Jackie Chan in
WHEELS ON MEALS

Jackie Chan in
WHEELS ON MEALS

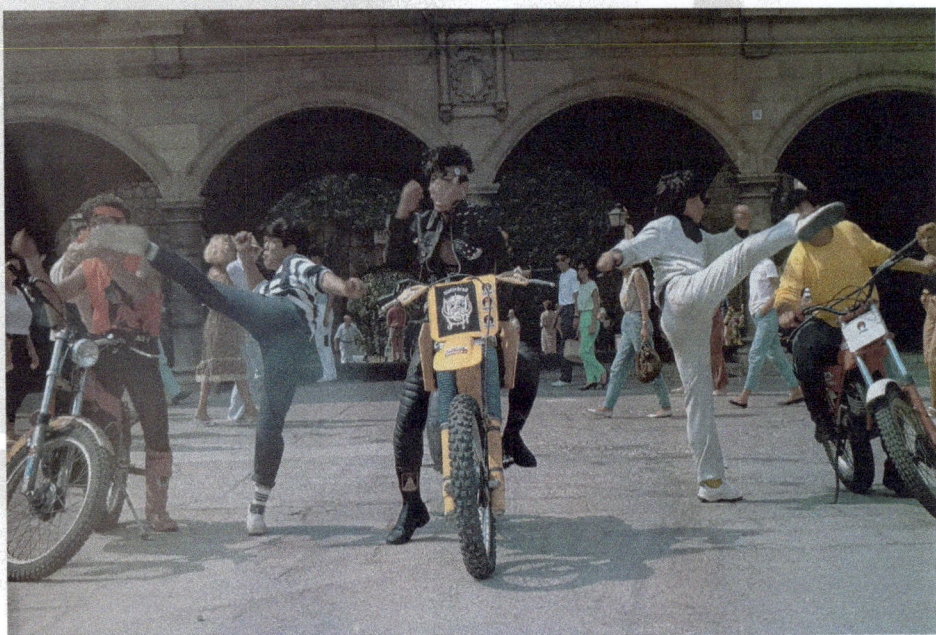

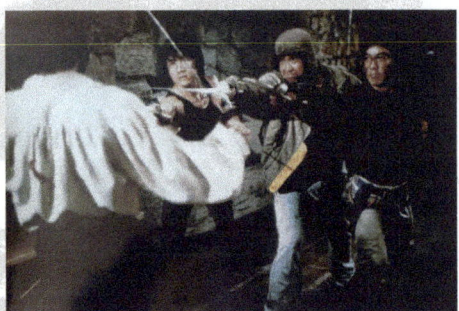

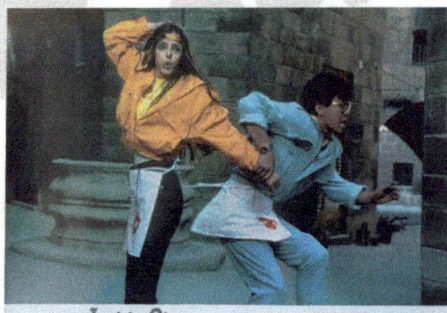

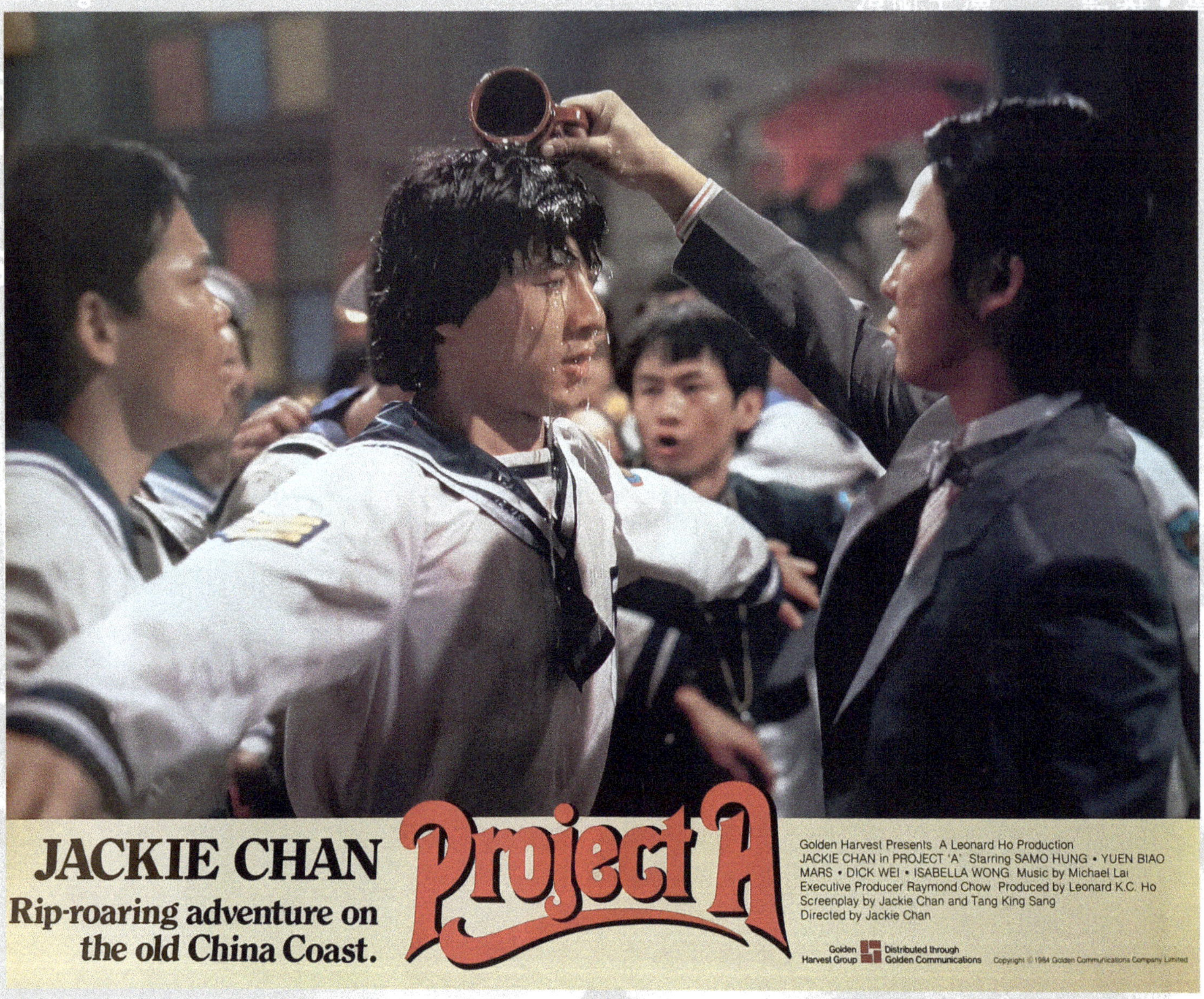
JACKIE CHAN
Rip-roaring adventure on the old China Coast.
Project A
Golden Harvest Presents A Leonard Ho Production
JACKIE CHAN in PROJECT 'A' Starring SAMO HUNG • YUEN BIAO
MARS • DICK WEI • ISABELLA WONG Music by Michael Lai
Executive Producer Raymond Chow Produced by Leonard K.C. Ho
Screenplay by Jackie Chan and Tang King Sang
Directed by Jackie Chan
Golden Harvest Group
Distributed through Golden Communications
Copyright © 1984 Golden Communications Company Limited

Project A
Is an action-comedy film directed by and starring Jackie Chan, alongside Sammo Hung and Yuen Biao. The film takes place in the late 19th century in Hong Kong and follows the adventures of three characters as they battle against pirates and corrupt officials.

The film features Jackie Chan as Sergeant Dragon Ma, a member of the Hong Kong Marine Police who is tasked with capturing the notorious pirate gang that is wreaking havoc in the city. Chan's performance as Sergeant Dragon Ma is outstanding, and he brings his signature brand of humor and action to the character. His martial arts skills are also on full display throughout the film, and his comedic timing is excellent.

Sammo Hung plays the role of Fei, a police officer who is Dragon's friend and colleague. Fei is a bit of a hot-headed character, and he often finds himself in trouble due to his impulsive nature. Sammo Hung's performance as Fei is excellent, and he brings a lot of energy to the film. His fight scenes are also incredibly well choreographed, and he showcases his impressive martial arts skills throughout the film.

Yuen Biao plays the role of Tien, a member of the Coast Guard who becomes involved in Dragon and Fei's mission to stop the pirates. Tien is a skilled fighter and is tasked with guarding the governor, who is being targeted by the pirates. Yuen Biao's performance as Tien is excellent, and he brings a lot of depth to the character. His fight scenes are also incredibly well choreographed, and he showcases his impressive martial arts skills throughout the film.

One of the film's most memorable scenes is when Jackie Chan engages in a high-flying battle on a clock tower. This scene is an excellent showcase of Chan's acrobatic and martial arts skills and sets the tone for the rest of the film. Additionally, the film's climactic battle scene, takes place on a pirate ship, with an incredible display of martial arts and action.

In conclusion, "Project A" is an excellent action-comedy film that showcases the impressive talents of Jackie Chan, Sammo Hung, and Yuen Biao. The film's fight scenes are incredibly well choreographed, and the performances of the three main characters are outstanding.

JACKIE CHAN

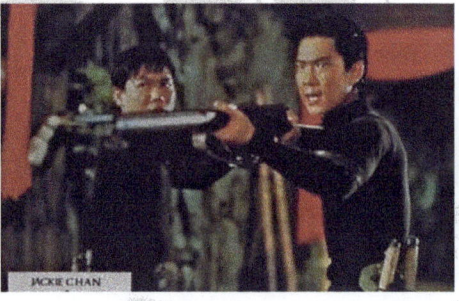

DRAGONS FOREVER

Is a 1988 Hong Kong action-comedy film directed by Sammo Hung, who also stars in the film alongside Jackie Chan and Yuen Biao. The movie tells the story of a lawyer named Jackie Lung (Jackie Chan), who is hired by a chemical factory owner to defend him against charges of polluting the local river. Jackie's investigation leads him to the doorstep of a ruthless businessman named Hua Hsien-Wu (Yuen Wah), who will stop at nothing to protect his illegal activities. Along the way, Jackie is aided by his friend Luke (Yuen Biao), a private investigator with an eye for the ladies.

Yuen Biao's performance in "Dragons Forever" is nothing short of outstanding. He delivers a nuanced and emotionally resonant portrayal of Luke, a character torn between his loyalty to Jackie and his growing attraction to Hua Hsien-Wu's mistress, played by Pauline Yeung. Yuen Biao's physical prowess is also on full display in the film's many action sequences, where he performs stunts and acrobatics that are as impressive as they are breathtaking.

Director Sammo Hung, who also choreographed the film's fight scenes, imbues "Dragons Forever" with a sense of playfulness and humor that is characteristic of his style. The fight scenes are expertly staged and choreographed, blending comedy and action in a way that feels organic and never forced. Hung's direction also brings out the best in his cast, allowing each actor to shine in their respective roles.

Of course, no discussion of "Dragons Forever" would be complete without mentioning Jackie Chan. As always, Chan is a delight to watch on screen, bringing his trademark blend of physical comedy and martial arts prowess to the role of Jackie Lung. Chan's chemistry with Yuen Biao and Sammo Hung is palpable, and their scenes together are some of the film's highlights.

Overall, "Dragons Forever" is a must-see for fans of Hong Kong action cinema. The film's stellar cast, expertly choreographed fight scenes, and playful sense of humor make it a standout in the genre. Yuen Biao and Sammo Hung's contributions to the film are particularly noteworthy, adding depth and nuance to an already impressive work of cinema.

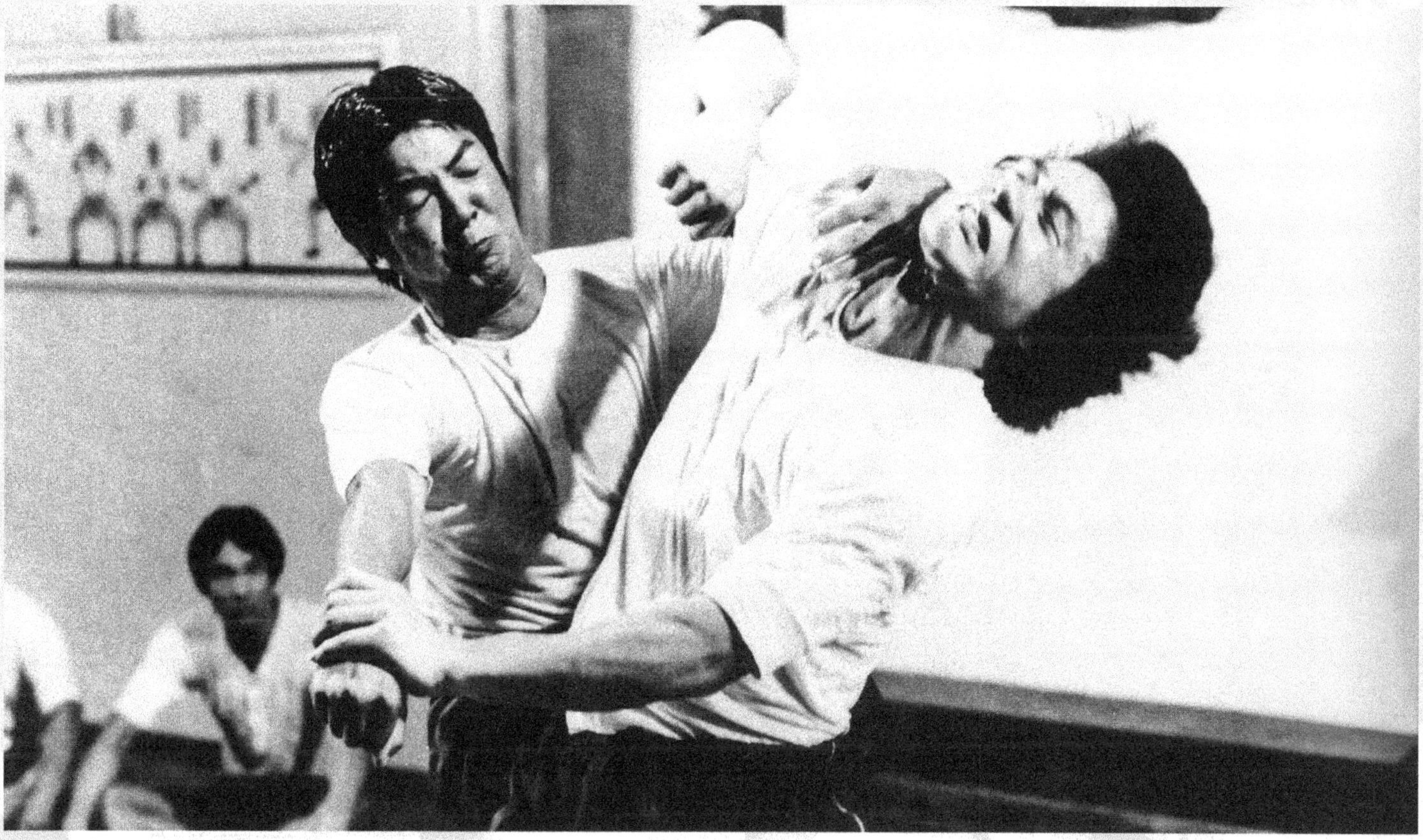

Page 75 Yuen Biao Special

COLLECTING JACKY CHAN JAPANESE LPs

By MICHAEL NESBITT

By the late 1970s, the Bruce Lee craze was on the decline, and already a new Asian Martial Arts Superstar was on the horizon, and that man was Jackie Chan. Compared to Bruce Lee, Jackie Chan was a different kind of martial arts movie star, whereas Bruce Lee was more serious and tried to incorporate realistic movements in his movies, Jackie used more slapstick comedy, entwined with acrobatic Kung Fu movements to excite the audience. By 1978, as Bruce Lee's decline was evident, Jackie's popularity was just beginning, and with the release of both Drunken Master and Snake in the Eagle Shadow, the fans flocked to the cinemas to see their new action hero.

Throughout the 1970s, Bruce Lee Japanese LPs were very popular with action movie fans, and as always, Japan was quick to capitalise on Jackie Chan's new-found stardom and began releasing Jackie Chan LPs. The two major differences between Bruce Lee Japanese vinyl's, and Jackie Chan's, were: 1- By the 1980s, Jackie had a lot more movies released than Bruce, meaning more soundtracks. And 2- Jackie Chan could actually sing. Jackie would often sing the soundtrack to his own movies, which made him a popular music star in Asia, and he even sang live at many concerts.

However, it wasn't until 1980 that the Japanese market released its first Jackie Chan LPs, with both throughout Japan. At the height of Jackie Chan's music career, in 1985, Japan released a total of nine Jackie Chan albums. However, like most things, it wasn't to last. With the popularity of the Compact Disc (CD) in the late 1980s, companies were releasing fewer vinyl albums, and in 1988, Elektra released Jackie Chan's final two albums, Hong Kong My Love and The Best of Jackie Chan. A total of 43 Jackie Chan albums were released in Japan, with the final two came the inevitable demise of the Japanese martial arts movie LP.

In today's market, Japanese vinyl LPs are highly collectable, and even more so if they still have their original OBI, a sash in Japanese which were originally named for the belts worn in traditional Japanese clothing. These OBIs would highlight the major selling points of the album, including No 1 hits, singers who collaborated on the album, or any free gifts like photos or posters which were included.

Title: Battle Creek Brawl
Year: 1980
Label: Victor
SIDE A1: Training Montage. **A2**: Fast Moves. **A3**: Uncle Herbert. **A4**: Playing Nurse. **A5**: Jerry's Rag. **A6**: The Trap.
SIDE B1: Training Montage. **B2**: Oriental Drama. **B3**: Roller Derby. **B4**: Razor Cuts. **B5**: Miss Wong. **B6**: The Kiss Of Death. **B7**: Victory Fanfare. **B8**: Training Montage.
Info: One insert. Soundtrack from the movie.

Title: The Young Master
Year: 1980
Label: Victor
SIDE A1: Theme From The Young Master. **A2**: Chasing The White Fan. **A3**: Variation From Peaceful Tune. **A4**: Kim's Fighting. **A5**: Son Of Officer Jaguar. **A6**: White Folding Fan.
SIDE B1: Spanish Kung Fu. **B2**: Kim's Theme. **B3**: Looking For Tiger. **B4**: Peaceful Tune. **B5**: Chan & Jaguar. **B6**: Final Match.
Info: One insert. Soundtrack from the movie.

Title: The Miracle Fist
Year: 1981
Label: Columbia
SIDE A1: Father's Avenge. **A2**: Heroes of the Republic. **A3**: China Girl - I'm Not Afraid of Youkai. **A4**: Five Beast Fists. **A5**: Press Conference - Broken Blossom.
SIDE B1: Drunk Hachisen - Amida's own Kenpo. **B2**: Snake Fist Teaching. **B3**: Crazy Monkey. **B4**: Monkey Man. **B5**: Crazy Monkey - Confrontation with Nin. **Info**: One insert.

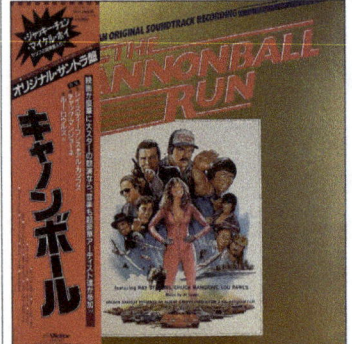

Title: The Cannonball Run
Year: 1981
Label: Victor
SIDE A1: Cannonball. **A2**: Here Come Da Sheik. **A3**: Love Is On The Air. **A4**: Beauty's Theme. **A5**: If And When. **A6**: Moore Of The Same.
SIDE B1: The Cannonball Run. **B2**: Just For The Hell Of It. **B3**: Hong King Kong. **B4**: T-T-Turn Left. **B5**: Captain Chaos Strikes. **B6**: You've Gotta Have A Dream.
Info: One insert.

Title: The Miracle Fist Part 2
Year: 1981
Label: Columbia
SIDE A1: Miracle Fighter. **A2**: Fengko and Zukoke Date. **A3**: Southern Breeze. **A4**: Interview Pt 1 and Pt 2. **A5**: Samhua Samtime.
SIDE B1: Technotech Kung Fu. **B2**: Become a Disciple rather than Drunken Boxing. **B3**: Interview Pt 3. **B4**: Snake Fist. **B5**: Interview Pt 4. **B6**: Fight Not Fight - Laughing Fist.
Info: One insert.

Title: : Dragon Fist
Year: 1982
Label: Columbia
SIDE A1: Dragon Fist. **A2**: A Pledge Of Revenge. **A3**: A Long Way To Go. **A4**: The Poisoned Tea. **A5**: Alone In The Night. **A6**: A Confession Of Chun. **A7**: Do Or Die.
SIDE B1: Caught In The Trap. **B2**: Trap. **B3**: Inconsistent Mind. **B4**: Alone In The Night (Long Version). **B5**: Suicide. **B6**: Last Battle. **B7**: Dragon Fist.
Info: One insert.

Title: Dragon Lord
Year: 1982
Label: Victor
SIDE A1: Dragon Lord. **A2:** Main Theme. **A3**: Doughball Game. **A4**: Discovery Of Sexy. **A5**: Fight With Cowboy. **A6**: The Shuttle-Cock Game.
SIDE B1: The Captain. **B2**: Let's Fly The Kite. **B3**: Discovery Of Sexy - Main Theme. **B4**: Chase. **B5**: Fight With The Captain. **B6**: The Joker Went Wild.
Info: One insert.

Title: Viva! Jackie Chan
Year: 1982
Label: Victor
SIDE A1: The Cannonball. **A2:** Cannonball Run. **A3**: Miracle Guy. **A4**: Broken Blossom. **A5**: Training Montage. **A6**: Playing Nurse. **A7**: China Girl.
SIDE B1: Theme from the Young Master. **B2**: Chasing the White Fan. **B3**: Looking For Tiger. **B4**: Lesson Of Kung Fu. **B5**: Kungfusion. **B6**: Suippasen. **B7**: Crazy Monkey.
Info: One insert.

Title: Songs For Jacky Chan (The Miracle Fist)
Year: 1982
Label: Columbia
SIDE A1: Fist Method Confusion. **A2**: Miracle Guy. **A3**: Do Oh Dai. **A4**: Crazy Monkey. **A5**: Alone in the Night. **A6**: China Girl.
SIDE B1: Dragon Fist. **B2**: Miracle Fighter. **B3**: Technotech Kung Fu. **B4**: Monkey Man. **B5**: Broken Blossom. **B6**: Samhua Samtime.
Info: One insert.

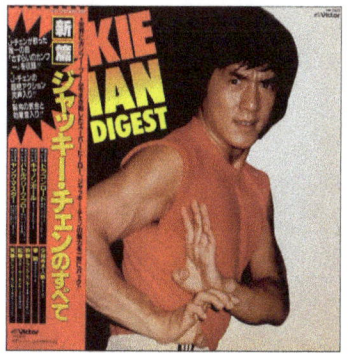

Title: Jackie Chan Digest
Year: 1983
Label: Victor
SIDE A1: Dragon Lord. **A2**: Jackie Chan Theme. **A3**: Cannonball Theme. **A4**: Miracle Guy. **A5**: Jackie Chan Theme. **A6**: Nancy Nursing. **A7**: Crazy Monkey.
SIDE B1: Wandering Kung Fu. **B2**: White Fan. **B3**: Looking for a Tiger. **B4**: China Girl. **B5**: Snake Shaped Fist Teaching. **B6**: Fist Confusion. **B7**: Drunk Hachisen.
Info: One insert. Tracks taken nine movies, including - Dragon Lord, Shaolin Wooden Men, The Fearless Hyena and Spiritual Kung Fu.

Title: The Dragon Attack (Fantasy Mission Force)
Year: 1983
Label: Phillips
SIDE A1: Birth of a Dragon Special Attack Corps. **A2**: Jackie Appeared. **A3**: Showdown! Escape from Amazones.
SIDE B1: Kamikaze Dreams. **B2**: Happening of the Ghost Mountain Lodge. **B3**: Warrior Rest. **B4**: Gekito! The Final Battle.
Info: One insert.

Title: Cunning Monkey (Half a Loaf of Kung Fu)
Year: 1983
Label: Columbia
SIDE A1: Cunning Monkey. **A2**: Secret Fist. **A3**: Tenchuken. **A4**: One Point Lesson of Hekkoki Futaro.
SIDE B1: Monkey's On the Loose. **B2**: Mysterious Medicine. **B3**: Tenchuken No.1. **B4**: Kung Fu Sister Appears. **B5**: The Final Blow.
Info: One insert.

Title: Cannonball Run II (Jackie Chan Deluxe)
Year: 1983
Label: Victor
SIDE A1: Power On. **A2**: Dragon Lord. **A3**: The Joker Went Wild. **A4**: Cannonball. **A5**: Miracle Guy. **A6**: Training Montage. **A7**: Playing Nurse.
SIDE B1: The Young Master Theme. **B2**: Chasing The White Fan. **B3**: China Girl. **B4**: Crazy Monkey. **B5**: Lesson of Kung Fu. **B6**: Kung Fusion. **B7**: The Master With Cracked Fingers Theme.
Info: One insert.

Title: Snake and Crane Arts of Shaolin
Year: 1983
Label: Columbia
SIDE A1: Dangerous Eyes. **A2**: The Strongest Fist (Instrument). **A3**: Snake and Crane Fighting (Piano Solo). **A4**: Dangerous Eyes (Instrument).
SIDE B1a: Snake and Crane Fighting (Instrument). **B1b**: The Strongest Fist (Instrument). **B2**: Dangerous Eyes (Piano Solo). **B3a**: The Moonless Night (Instrument). **B3b**: Dangerous Eyes.
Info: One insert.

Title: Jackie Chan Perfect Collection
Year: 1983
Label: Columbia
SIDE A1: Cunning Monkey. **A2**: Dangerous Eyes. **A3**: Crazy Monkey. **A4**: Confusion Constitution. **A5**: Dragon Fist. **A6**: Miracle Fighter.
SIDE B1: Miracle Guy. **B2**: China Girl. **B3**: Monkey, Eagle's Shadow. **B4**: The Cannonball. **B5**: Training Montage. **B6**: Dragon Lord. **B7**: Theme from The Young Master.
Info: One insert.

Title: Songs For Jackie Chan
Year: 1984
Label: Columbia
SIDE A1: To Kill with Intrigue. **A2:** Project A. **A3**: Cannonball 2. **A4**: Danger Love. **A5**: Canning Monkey. **A6**: Cannonball Theme. **A7**: Dragon Lord.
SIDE B1: Dangerous Eyes. **B2**: Marianne. **B3**: Wandering Kung Fu. **B4**: Dragon Fist. **B5**: China Girl. **B6**: Miracle Guy. **B7**: Miracle Fighter.
Info: One insert. Picture Disc.

Title: Collection Of Trailers & Main Theme Songs
Year: 1984
Label: Columbia
SIDE A1: To Kill with Intrigue. **A2:** The Dragon Attack. **A3**: The Fearless Hyena. **A4**: Spiritual Kung Fu. **A5**: Shaolin Wooden Men.
SIDE B1: Half A Loaf of Kung Fu. **B2**: Snake & Crane Arts Of Shaolin. **B3**: Snake In The Eagle Shadow. **B4**: Dragon Fist. **B5**: Drunken Master In The Tiger's Eye.
Info: Two inserts.

Title: Jackie Chan New Special
Year: 1984
Label: Victor
SIDE A1: Project A. **A2**: Power On. **A3**: Theme From The Young Master. **A4**: Chasing The White Fan.
SIDE B1: Dragon Lord. **B2**: Main Theme From Dragon Lord. **B3**: Training Montage. **B4**: Project A (Male Chorus).
Info: Two inserts. Picture Disc.

Title: Love Me
Year: 1984
Label: Elektra
SIDE A1: Movie Star. **A2**: Jackie's Legend. **A3**: Marianne. **A4**: Tell Me Again.
SIDE B1: Love Me. **B2**: In April. **B3**: Hello Happy Song. **B4**: Wait For Me.
Info: Three Inserts.

Title: Many Thanks
Year: 1984
Label: Elektra
SIDE A1: Marianne (Cantonese version). **A2:** Hello Happy Song (Cantonese version).
SIDE B1: Project A (Cantonese version). **B2**: Project A (Karaoke).
Info: One insert. This is a 12in, 45 RPM, EP, Limited Edition, Picture Disc.

Title: Project A
Year: 1984
Label: Victor
SIDE A1: Project A - Vocals Jackie Chan. **A2**: The Symphony No.5 Of Beethoven. **A3**: Attention! **A4**: The Pirates. **A5**: Any Time. **A6**: At the VIP Club. **A7**: Sad Mood and Dragon's Joke.
SIDE B1: The Chase. **B2**: Beating the Retreat. **B3**: The Raid In The Dark. **B4**: Diving from the Clock Tower. **B5**: Project A - Proceeds. **B6**: The Last Duel In The Island. **B7**: Project A (Male Chorus).
Info: Two inserts.

Title: The Lucky 5 Stars (Winners & Sinners)
Year: 1984
Label: Canyon
SIDE A1: Super Superstar. **A2**: The 5 Lucky Stars. **A3**: Super Superstar. **A4**: Mafia Corps Meet. **A5**: Godfather - Source Theme. **A6**: Super Superstar. **A7**: Angel.
SIDE B1: Super Superstar. **B2**: Get back the original Godfather. **B3**: Mafia Corps Attendance. **B4**: Winners & Sinners. **B5**: Super Superstar. **B6**: The 5 Lucky Stars. **B7**: Angel. **B8**: Angel.
Info: One insert. Tracks with the same name are variations mainly with narration.

Title: To Kill with Intrigue
Year: 1984
Label: Columbia
SIDE A1: To Kill with Intrigue (Theme Song). **A2**: Revenge of the Bee Party. **A3**: Somewhere Far Away. **A4**: Ryushi's Confession. **A5**: I Never Said It's Forever Song.
SIDE B1: Blood Rain Party Counterattack. **B2**: Crisis of Lightning. **B3**: The Identity of Kanagawa - The Death of Ryushi. **B4**: In Search of Thousands Days of Hardship. **B5**: Fierce Fight! To Kill with Intrigue.
Info: One insert. Picture disc.

Title: Spartan X (Wheels on Meals)
Year: 1984
Label: Victor
SIDE A1: Spartan X. **A2**: At the Barcelona's. **A3**: The Chase. **A4**: Theme Of Money. **A5**: Battle of Old Castle. **A6**: The Chase in Barcelona's. **A7**: Silvia's Confession.
SIDE B1: Theme From Spartan X. **B2**: The Invader. **B3**: Silvia's Theme. **B4**: In the Mental Hospital. **B5**: Disco Scene. **B6**: The Death Match. **B7**: At the Dinner Party.
Info: One insert.

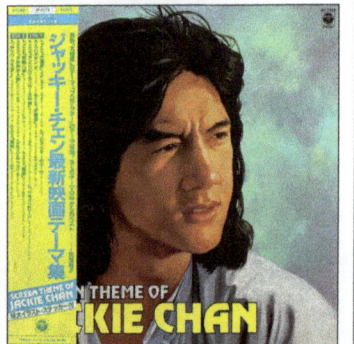

Title: Screen Theme of Jackie Chan
Year: 1985
Label: Columbia
SIDE A1: Good Luck Overture (Theme of Daifukusei). **A2**: The Protector Theme (instrumental). **A3**: Spartan X (Instrumental). **A4**: To Kill with Intrigue. **A5**: Canning Monkey. **A6**: Dragon Lord.
SIDE B1: Dangerous Eyes. **B2**: Dragon Fist. **B3**: Miracle Guy. **B4**: Miracle Fighter. **B5**: Wandering Kung Fu. **B6**: China Girl.
Info: One insert.

Title: Dear Jackie
Year: 1985
Label: Elektra
Side A: Dear Jackie.
Side B1: Primadonna at Dawn. **B2**: Dear Jackie (Instrumental).
Info: One insert. This is a 12 inch, 45 RPM, Maxi-Single.

Title: Jackie Chan - The Great Fight
Year: 1985
Label: Seven Seas
SIDE A1: The Protector (Main Theme). **A2**: The Protector - One Up for the Good Guys. **A3**: Project A. **A4**: Spartan X. **A5**: The Young Master, (Theme). **A6**: Crazy Monkey.
SIDE B1: The Cannonball 2 - Power On. **B2**: Dragon Lord. **B3**: Dragon Lord - The Joker Went Wild. **B4**: The Cannonball - Cannonball. **B5**: The Cannonball - Cannonball Run. **B6**: Battle Creek Brawl - Training Montage.
Info: Two inserts, one folds out into a large poster.

Title: Daifukusei (My Lucky Stars)
Year: 1985
Label: Canyon
SIDE A1: Hong Kong Express. **A2**: S.O.S from Tokyo. **A3**: My Lucky Star I. **A4**: Farewell Baikal. **A5**: Raid of the Masked Group.
SIDE B1: Good Luck - Overture. **B2**: My Lucky Star II. **B3**: Flower My Love. **B4**: Kung Fu Star. **B5**: Shining Daifukusei.
Info: Two inserts.

Title: Police Story
Year: 1985
Label: Victor
SIDE A1: Theme from the Police Story. **A2**: Happy Birthday, Chan! **A3**: Mystery and Suspect. **A4**: Chan Bluffs on the Telephone. **A5**: Suspend to Chase. **A6**: Sexy Tape. **A7**: Funny Meeting with Salena.
SIDE B1: Fighting in the Bus. **B2**: Chan in on the Phones. **B3**: Jackie Chan Dialog - Chan's Rebellion. **B4**: The Hostage. **B5**: The Grand Fight. **B6**: Theme from The Police Story (Sound Effects).
Info: One insert.

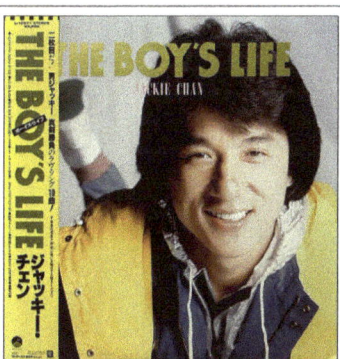

Title: This Boy's Life
Year: 1985
Label: Elektra
SIDE A1: Tokyo Saturday Night. **A2**: China Blue. **A3**: Wow Wow Wow. **A4**: Memories of Eagles. **A5**: Try To Love Me.
SIDE B1: I Love You, You, You. **B2**: Intuition Platonic. **B3**: Good Night in my Chest. **B4**: Hong Kong Twilight. **B5**: Rose-coloured Eyes.
Info: Comes with an insert, lyric booklet, and sticker sheet.

Title: : The Protector
Year: 1985
Label: Seven Seas
SIDE A1: The Protector (Main Title). **A2**: Hijacking the Truck. **A3**: Cocktails Anyone? **A4**: Welcome to New York? **A5**: Hotel Shoot Out. **A6**: The Warehouse.
SIDE B1: Texan Truck Driver. **B2**: Hong Kong Harbour. **B3**: Massage For Two. **B4**: The Temple. **B5**: Lee Hing Escapes. **B6**: The Final Confrontation. **B7**: One Up For The Good Guys.
Info: One insert.

Title: The First Mission
Year: 1985
Label: Elektra
SIDE A1: China Blue (Remix). **A2**: Action A. **A3**: Heart of Dragon. **A4**: Tokyo Saturday Night (Instrumental). **A5**: China Blue.
SIDE B1: Heart of Dragon (Reprise). **B2**: Action B. **B3**: Brother Theme. **B4**: China Blue (Instrumental). **B5**: Action C. **B6**: Tokyo Saturday Night.
Info: One insert.

Title: Prelude from the Protector
Year: 1985
Label: Victor
SIDE A1: Protector - Overture. **A2**: Project A. **A3** Power On. **A4**: Cannonball Theme. **A5**: Dragon Lord. **A6**: Jackie Chan's Theme. **A7**: Miracle Guy.
SIDE B1: Spartan X. **B2**: Wandering Kung Fu. **B3**: Fist Confusion. **B4**: Snake Shaped Fist Teaching. **B5**: Crazy Monkey. **B6**: China Girl. **B7**: Special Iron Finger Fist Theme.
Info: One insert. Soundtracks taken from The Protector and other Jackie Chan Movies.

Title: Hong Kong Explosion
Year: 1985
Label: Canyon
SIDE A1: Lucky Theme (From My Lucky Stars). **A2**: Kung Fu Star. **A3**: Saraba Bikaru "Goodbye Bikaru" (From My Lucky Stars). **A4**: Super Superstar. **A5**: Angel.
SIDE B1: Champion Hawk (From The Champions). **B2**: Lonely Player (From Drunken Monkey). **B3**: Kung Fu Confusion (From Drunken Monkey). **B4**: The Tipsy Dandy (The Drunken Monkey). **B5**: Return of the Dragon (From Fist of Fury)
Info: One 4 sided insert. A compilation of music taken from various Hong Kong movies. Two of the songs on the album are sung by Yuen Biao.

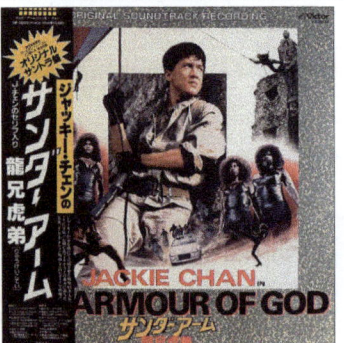

Title: Armour of God
Year: 1986
Label: Victor
SIDE A1: The Balloon. **A2**: Tribal Drums. **A3** You Must Wait For Me. **A4**: The Messages. **A5**: The Escape. **A6**: The Fight.
SIDE B1: Jackie's Escape. **B2**: The Drugging of Lorelei. **B3**: The Auction. **B4**: Jackie Fights Back. **B5**: Beware of the Dogs. **B6**: The Market. **B7**: The Explosion.
Info: One insert.

Title: Jackie Chan's Awakening Fist (Fearless Hyena 2)
Year: 1986
Label: Canyon
SIDE A1: First Blood. **A2**: Hop, Step, Champ I. **A3** Adventure King. **A4**: Awakening Fist Fighting. **A5**: Legend of The Brothers.
SIDE B1: Ichibanboshi Boogie. **B2**: Hop, Step, Champ II. **B3**: Wake Up! Awakening Fist. **B4**: Return of the Great Arms. **B5**: Last Blood.
Info: One insert.

Title: Shangri-La
Year: 1986
Label: Elektra
SIDE A1: Love Again. **A2**: Just Me. **A3** A Night that Suits Slowdown. **A4**: Just For Tonight. **A5**: Esperance.
SIDE B1: Only For Your Love. **B2**: Don't Stop Romance. **B3**: Hello from the Back. **B4**: Become a Storm - Featuring Anita Mui. **B5**: August Carmen.
Info: One insert.

Title: No Problem
Year: 1987
Label: Elektra
SIDE A1: Telephone. **A2**: Stardust Bay Blues. **A3**: Jealousy Rains. **A4**: Miss Temptation. **A5**: Gorgeousness.
SIDE B1: No Problem. **B2**: Tears of Jade. **B3**: Maria My Love. **B4**: Dream Ties.
Info: One insert.

Title: Project A Part 2
Year: 1987
Label: Victor
SIDE A1: The Project A2 March. **A2**: Pink Dress. **A3**: Waltz. **A4**: Veil of Conspiracy. **A5**: Leave it to Jackie. **A6**: Confrontation Largest-eve. **A7**: Project A: Attack Instruction of Jackie.
SIDE B1: Project A2 Take 2. **B2**: Project A. **B3**: Tiger of the West Ring. **B4**: Flight. **B5**: Surprise Attack. **B6**: Plot of Jackie. **B7**: Revenge of the Shark. **B8**: The Aim of the Emissary. **B9**: Immortal Jackie.
Info: One insert.

Title: Seven Lucky Stars (Twinkle Twinkle Lucky Stars)
Year: 1987
Label: Elektra
SIDE A1: Main Title. **A2**: Killers Attack. **A3**: No problem (Action Version). **A4**: Seven Lucky Stars (Part I). **A5**: Kid & Flower.
SIDE B1: No Problem (Theme Song). **B2**: Unbalance. **B3**: Seven Lucky Stars (Part II). **B4**: Hong Kong Police. **B5**: Last Fighting.
Info: One insert.

	**Title**: Cyclone Z (Dragons Forever) **Year**: 1988 **Label**: Victor **SIDE A1**: Theme from Cyclone Z. **A2**: Open Air Coffee Shop. **A3**: Yuen Biao Appears. **A4**: Dinner for Two. **A5**: Sammo Goes to Jackie's House. **A6**: Walking Outside. **SIDE B1**: Theme from Cyclone Z (Instrumental). **B2**: Romance Fisher. **B3**: Yuen Biao Bugs House. **B4**: Fight Scene. **B5**: Discotheque Bar. **B6**: The Battle in the Factory. **Info**: One insert.
	**Title**: Hong Kong My Love **Year**: 1988 **Label**: Elektra **SIDE A1**: Tsim Sha Tsui - Super Class Night. **A2**: Love Serenade (Cantonese Version). **A3**: Southern Cruise (Cantonese Version). **SIDE B1**: Marika's Love. **B2** Police Story 2 - Kowloon Eyes (Hong Kong Version Theme Song). **B3**: O-Y-A-S-U-M-I. **Info**: One insert. This is a Mini-Album
	**Title**: The Best of Jackie Chan **Year**: 1988 **Label**: Elektra **SIDE A1**: Marika's Love. **A2**: Marianne. **A3**: Project A. **A4**: Movie Star. **A5**: No Problem. **A6**: Thunder Arm - Brother Tiger Brother Theme Song (Unreleased Japanese Arrangement Version). **SIDE B1**: I Love You, You, You. **B2** Heart is Yes. **B3**: Just For Tonight. **B4**: Love Serenade (Cantonese Version). **B5**: Tokyo Saturday Night. **Info**: One insert.

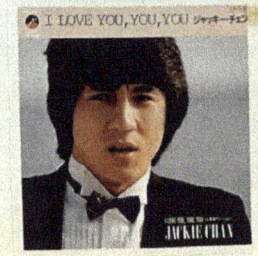

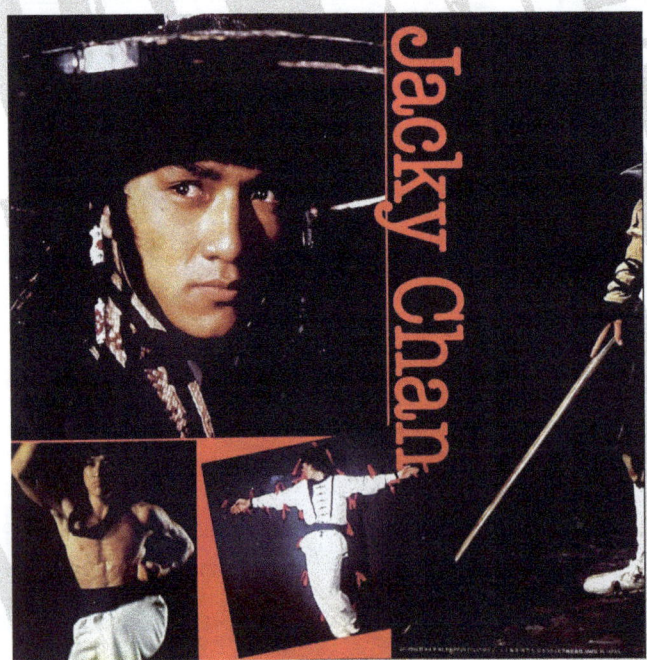

The Eccentric Swordsman: Yuen Biao in...

龍鳳賊捉賊
LICENSE TO STEAL

Review by Shazad Asghar

License to Steal aka *Licence to Steal*, is a 1990 film produced by Sammo Hung and directed by Billy Chan Wui-Ngai. It stars Joyce Godenzi, Richard Ng, Ngai Sing (aka Colin Chou), Billy Chow and Yuen Biao. Please note I will be referring mainly to the character Biao plays in this film (Swordsman). Another look at this film was in an Eastern Heroes issue from last year. I had started this article a while back and hadn't realised it had been covered.

In *Dragons Forever*, Yuen Biao played a neurotic, ever so slightly unbalanced,

character seemingly struggling with his role in the world and appearing quite lonely. The character's name is Tung Te-Biao. At least one scene explaining his motivation later on in the film was a deleted scene, or originally only in international sversions of the film. I haven't returned to it for a while now, but I always found it hilarious the way he was so driven, yet confused, in that film. Some people have described the character's actions as psychotic at points, which seems a bit unfair. He is fiercely loyal to his friends, feels he's been betrayed, and even trying to see his therapist doesn't help (a criminal is giving advice from his therapist's office). Some of his actions from that point are a bit extreme. He seems to overthink every element of life. At one point he attempts to explain the political systems of birds and fish to Jackie Chan's character. His friends humour him for the most part. The scene at the bar where he stares at the criminals with utter hate, shows he is an idealist who does not want to mix with low life thugs. Despite being willing to plant bugs or other surveillance devices to help his friends! It's almost as if his character from Righting Wrongs had some kind of 'spiritual awakening' at some point, or visited a festival and had a bad trip. A very bad trip.

In Licence to Steal, he has a relatively small part, as 'Swordsman', the swordplay novel/wu xia obsessed nephew of Richard Ng's character. At one point in the film, Cory Yuen (in a small role as a policeman working under Richard Ng, aka Inspector Ta, aka Number One) describes Swordsman as "...a wizard versed in civil and military arts." After Biao's character leaves them, he adds, "A swordplay novel fan yearning to become a swordsman."

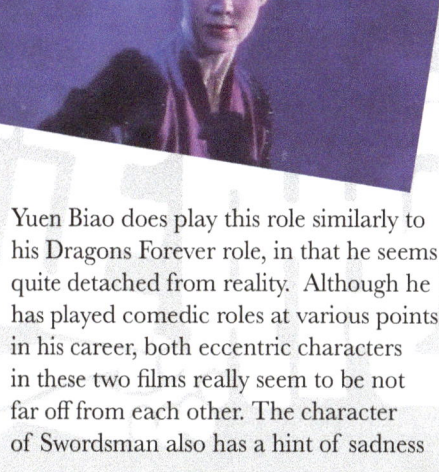

Yuen Biao does play this role similarly to his Dragons Forever role, in that he seems quite detached from reality. Although he has played comedic roles at various points in his career, both eccentric characters in these two films really seem to be not far off from each other. The character of Swordsman also has a hint of sadness behind the eccentricity, similar to his Dragons Forever role, with Dragons only having been released two years before Licence. The character of Swordsman seems to be disappointed with modern life, or is seeking escape in the values and traditions of the novels he consumes. Of course, being played by Biao, both characters are able to fight to an extremely high standard, and pull off acrobatic stunts seemingly effortlessly. Far from just being a fantasist, with the skills he admires confined to the fiction that he consumes, he is actually capable of performing. The only problem is he is slightly detached from reality, attempting to aid a police force who are trying to avoid him at the best of times, including his uncle, Inspector Ta/Number One.

Ngai Sing (aka Colin Chou) was mentored by Sammo Hung, and in this film accompanies the Inspector everywhere, as members of CID. The main plot of the film concerns a clan of thieves, headed by an Uncle Ting. He has raised three girls, who would work for him to commit raids of valuable objects, or whatever mission is given to them. The three women are Hung (Joyce Godenzi), Ngan (Agnes Aurelio) and Hsiao Yen (Alvina Kong Yan-Yin). At the start of the film we see Hung and Ngan sparring in a sword fight, setting up the rivalry between them that forms the backbone of the story. Optical discs (the size of a mini CD), that are used to select and decode the targets in their missions, will be an important part of the story. At one point in the film, Uncle Ting states, "The world of thieves is a mystery syndicate; syndicates everywhere, including us, deal through the use of codes."

Although genre films have always featured explicit language and themes, I should probably point out that during scene where the two female leads insult each other, Godenzi's character uses a severe racial insult. Think more like a Tarantino film. It is striking because the film is mostly quite light-hearted in tone, and although it was filmed three decades ago, some viewers might well be surprised. It could be due to the translation, and I am not overly sensitive to language in a film, but Sammo Hung's Don't Give a Damn would later feature much more of these kinds of insults.

Hung intends to leave the 'family' business, but ends up incarcerated. While she is gone her rival in the clan forms her own gang, with Billy Chow and some other heavies following her, and even disrespects their 'father.' Later, Hung will want her revenge, and the police also intend to use her against her 'sister.'

When we first see Swordsman/Biao, he dramatically jumps into the frame, wind blasting everywhere, with a fitting musical backing, as he says the classic line, "It smells of VICE here." The camera shows an exhaust pipe nearby, more likely the cause of the vice-like odour. When a tourist asks him to take a picture, he spots a pickpocket trying to steal from a woman near a coach. He intervenes, but she thinks

Swordsman is trying to steal her money, and they have a quick duel. She is played by Yeung Ching-Ching, who featured in many Shaw Brothers films, and also was a presenter of Dragons of the Orient (1988), a documentary featuring Fan Siu Wong, amongst others (she is also credited as the martial arts director). This is a great scene featuring her and Biao. He is amazed by a series of backflips she nails, as tourists cheer her performance. Before leaving, she tells him that to stand a chance against her, he should "practice more in Hua Shan." Swordsman is seriously impressed by her skill, and saddened that she leaves so soon.

Before Biao intervenes in a hostage situation, Cory Yuen adds that, "His language seems to be focused on honour, it's like he's a character in the novels he reads." Mistaking the hostage for a criminal, Swordsman shouts, "You bandit, you've raped and plundered. Fire at me, at my head and my heart!" Our hero then assaults the victim, who has a gun placed to the back of his spine, and can't move a muscle.

Later we see a short fight between Ngai Sing and Biao. They are both elite performers, of course, and it's a shame that this scene isn't much longer. There are other short fights, including outdoor stunts featuring a zip line escape, machine guns, motorbikes and many more, as well as break-ins and heists. The film features a lot of outdoor scenes, with city life mixed with some greenery. Occasionally, a plane might land in the near background, while characters converse on a rooftop.

The largest fight scene is in a multi-storey car park near the climax of the film. It is less well-lit compared to a similar scene in Righting Wrongs, but is arguably more complex than that sequence, pretty much equally brutal, and is up there in the car park fight rankings, with Burning Ambition following close behind. The scene starts with a mad dash between several cars, with the police in one car, Ngai Sing taking shots at the villains. This is where Billy Chow and the other villains all converge. Joyce initially takes on Chow, and then Biao appears to fight Chow. Ngai Sing takes on several crooks at a time, pulling off swift kicks and really going for it, no doubt about it. The stuntmen take some really painful-looking hits and falls. Biao and Chow's fight ends extremely painfully for the latter. It's probably mentioned whenever the film is discussed.

Although there is a finale after this car park battle, with Godenzi dressed in a very fancy suit, the car park is the highlight of the film. It is a very entertaining film, with a great cast and crew, comedy, stunts and action. Sadly, it's another film that is impossible to purchase in an official release, for now. There have previously been VHS, VCD and LaserDisc releases. An English dub is also known to exist. While not quite reaching the heights of the best output of these action stars, License to Steal is arguably just a level below their best work.

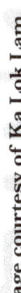

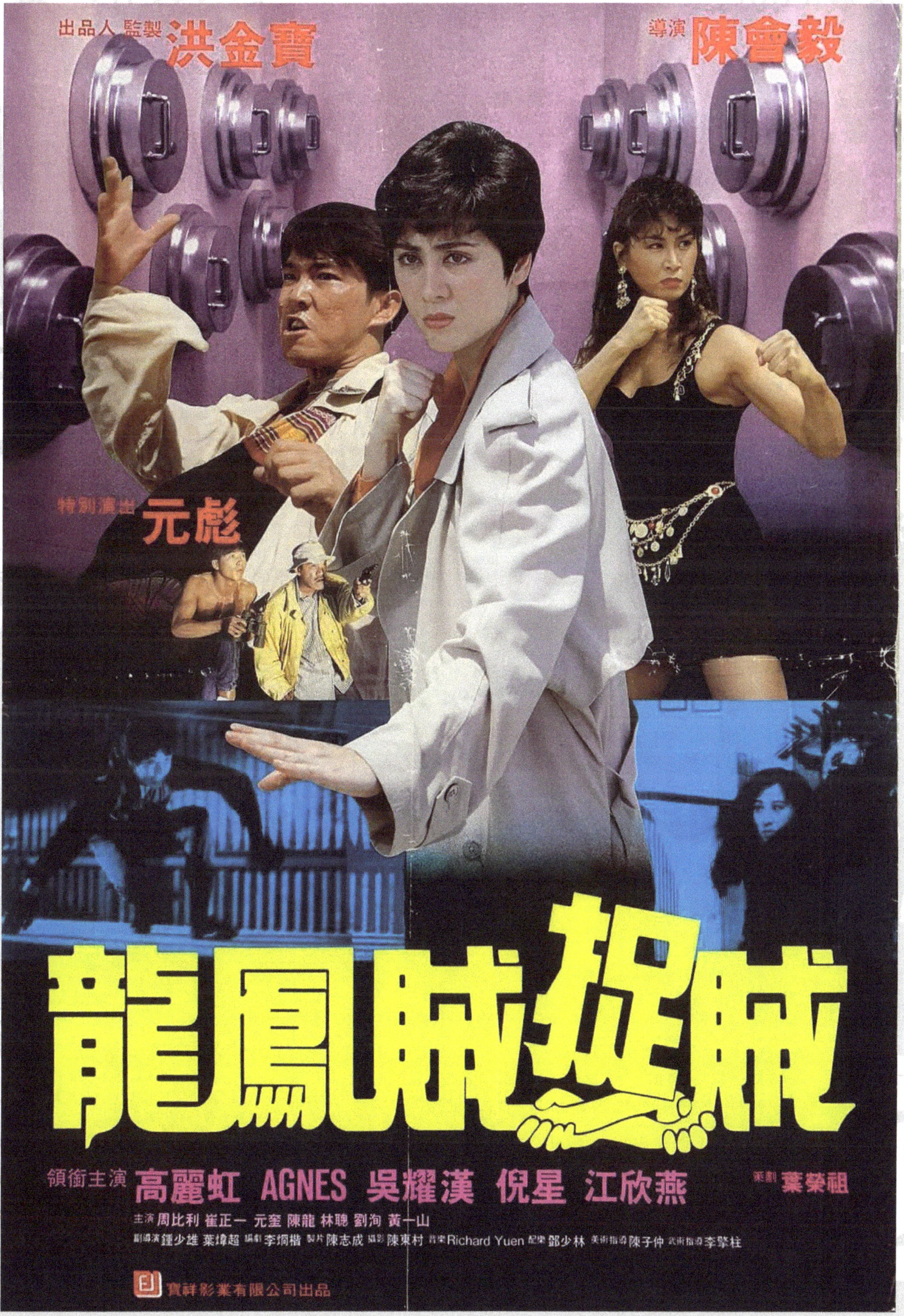

Image courtesy of Ka Lok Lam

Righting the Wrongs

A Look at a Selection of Yuen Biao's Film Posters with Alan Donkin and Matt Routledge

For years, Yuen Biao was one of those stars that I'd heard about in passing, but never specifically recognised. Genre fans a billion times more knowledgeable than me mentioned his name with hushed reverence, speaking of him with a dewy-eyed appreciation normally reserved for only the elite level performers. His name would be accompanied by phrases laced with superlatives, and nodding heads would allude to his underappreciation in the fanbase. It led to a feeling of guilt – I was one of the chumps who didn't really know anything about him. I mean, had I even seen him in a film? I didn't have a clue. Before long, another feeling started to surface. Curiosity. I've always had a keen interest in the underdog who just didn't get the same accolades as their peers, but was definitely deserving of respect. The cricketer who didn't play in a team of all talents, but should be considered a member in the pantheon of greats. The hockey player whose achievements couldn't be measured statistically, but was the driving force behind the charge to a Stanley Cup. The barely-known author, whose impressive body of work has lain neglected for years.

Why didn't I really know about Yuen Biao? The answer, I soon discovered, lay in the trajectory of his career. It clashed totally with my film preferences. Up until relatively recently, I didn't really 'do' the new wave stuff. Or the heroic bloodshed stuff. I was strictly old school. Shapes, wuxia and bashers. The more modern the setting, the more turned off I was. In an astonishing effort to machete off my own nose to spite my face, I wouldn't touch a modern setting with a bargepole. Guns and martial arts? Never the twain shall meet. Motorbikes and cars mixing with shapes? Don't be daft. That's not realistic. And martial arts films, especially old school ones, are all about realism, aren't they? Even typing this, my face is contorting in a 'what in the name of ... was I thinking?' way.

It's always been the case. My academic background is in history, and up until the age of 20, I wasn't interested in any topic too modern. If it was in living memory, forget it. I blame Harryhausen. He instilled a sense of wonder about the distant past within me from a young age. It seemed magical, yet still grounded in the reality of modern-looking people leaving behind stuff you could actually touch. A long gone past, both abstract and tangible. It was the same with kung fu films. I wanted to see things from hundreds of years ago, with the elaborate outfits, flamboyant fighting styles, codes of honour, and concepts just outside the confines of reality. Like the ability to reverse-jump up a fifty foot tree.

Yuen Biao had, I discovered, performed in plenty of 1970s old school films. Usually, though, it was in the role of an extra, or a stuntman, or a minor thug in a rumble. Hi ascent into leading parts didn't really kick on until the late 70s, and more prominently in the 1980s. Most of those roles were in bargepole films. Cursing my stupidity, I've started to correct the oversights of my stubbornness and ignorance. He's certainly one of the reasons that I've started to explore the 1980s modern-setting stuff with an open mind.

However, my former intransigence has led to a problem. When Rick asked if I'd like to do a piece for this special, I was two minds. I've watched a lot of his output from the 1980s, when he was part of the major core group of the cast, but the poster art accompanying his films leaves me stone cold. Bar a few exceptions that I looked at in the Jackie and Sammo magazines, they just don't click with me at all. I haven't yet reached the point where my openness

The 14 Amazons

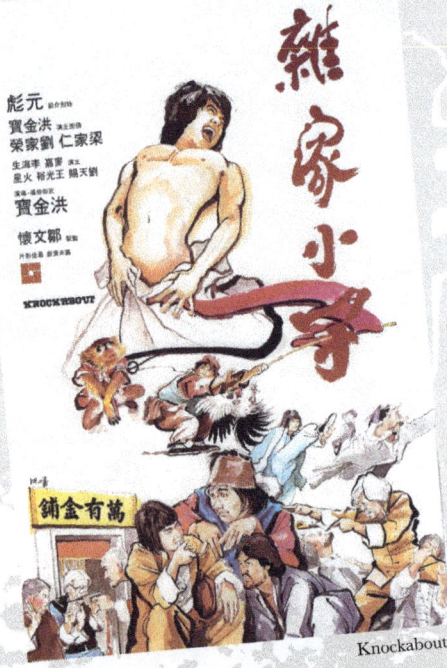

Knockabout

Freedom Strikes a Blow

Invincible Armour

The magic Blade

to the films transfers to an appreciation of photo-heavy 1980s poster art, usually featuring guns. After weeks of wondering what I could actually say, I decided to throw caution to the wind and look at the poster art from his movies regardless of his status inside the film. They are still films featuring Yuen Biao, no matter how modest his contribution. Vast swathes of his filmography shouldn't be purged from consideration just because he played 'troublemaker at tavern' rather than a headlining role.

I still couldn't force myself to look at the new wave 1980s posters with anything other than a disinterested an unappreciative eye, though, so I've asked my much-valued writing partner Matt to contribute a section about those. Consider it a duel. Old School vs New Wave. Biao's output as a minor star compared to his output as a major star. Matt can try and convince me that I'm missing out on a lot by rejecting a vast section of 1980s poster art.

The Best of the Old School
I'll say off the bat that I don't intend to dwell too much on posters that I've looked at in other issues. I want to use this opportunity to present some fascinating poster artwork that I haven't covered before.

Freedom Strikes a Blow (1973)
A Michael Chan Wai-Man and Bolo Yeung flick, this features Yuen Biao in the much-discussed role of 'extra'. A wise man once described 1980s poster art as 'photo heavy', so what gives? Surely this commits the cardinal sin that is the key feature of such mockery? Well, no. Michael Chan's photo does take up the majority of the piece, but look beyond it. The figure in front of him is hand-drawn in that wonderful style that seemed to characterise the late 1960s/early 70s era. Every feature is just clear enough to be recognisable, but vague enough to suggest movement and energy. The lighting on the trousers is superb, bringing the sketch to life, and providing the colour for the background in the upper half of the poster. The colour arrangement is very simple. White and blue, with Chan's dark hair matching the black elements featured in the mid-section backdrop. The simplicity is its strength. It isn't over-complicated or fussy – there's just a key trio of balanced colours. The red title and pink text ensure that key information is effectively presented for the cinemagoer. The only part of the poster I don't like is the awful font at the top. Utter dross, and distracts from a very modest, though effective, piece of poster artwork.

Wits to Wits (1974)

Another 'extra' role for Yuen Biao, in this martial arts comedy starring Henry Yu Yang, Sek Kin and Wu Ma.
Ever the hypocrite, this is actually set in the twentieth century, and features shootouts. It was 1970s efforts such as this that contributed to my realisation that self-imposed rules were absurd. Anyway, onto the poster. Again, we have hand-drawn art of the highest quality, skilfully presenting the relationship between the major characters. Not only are their expressions amazingly-sketched, but their bodies, hands and clothing are fantastic.
The background is very warm and bright, yet at the same time understated, thrusting the characters to prominence, without swallowing them up in garish chaos. The gradation from yellow to orange looks lovely, and the pink title text really complements it. Even the three black and white cast photos at the bottom look great. They ensure representation without overwhelming the design. The only thing I'm not fond of is the blue English text. It just gets a bit lost in the glow of everything else. A simple solution would have been to border the letters in another colour, making them stand out more. Shame.

The Master of Kung Fu (1973)
A Shaw Brothers entry about Wong Fei Hung, starring Ku Feng and Chen Ping. Yuen Biao features as one of Ku Feng's students. I've came across a couple of posters for this film. Both have merits and issues.
Variant One (an original effort on my part, that one) has a stunning red background, complete with black streaks like the coat of a tiger, or the scratches of a lion. It's really effective. The yellow text bordered by black is also striking, and the fonts generally work. There's a great action shot by our protagonist, and some nice action in the bottom corner. Granted, it's all photographs, but they are well-chosen and reflect the tone of the film effectively. My only issue with the poster is that massive head from the lion dance. It's a great design, but I don't know why it needs such prominence. It's only in the film in the first five minutes. It's just a matter of personal preference – I don't think that it suits the rest of the poster. The colours are too busy in an image that's already busy enough.

Talking of busy, Variant Two is a perfect example of a poster that tries to do too much. There are too many things happening in the design. Too many people doing different things. Taken as individual elements, they're all perfectly fine, especially the lion dance, which, in spite of it taking up the bulk of the image, is presented in a more careful manner. The lion is twisted, reducing the more overbearing aspects of its colours, in favour of shadow and muted tones. The action shot at the top is fine, as is the exchange in the middle. But thrown together, there's a general sense of chaos and overloading. I'm also not a fan of the yellow background and red circles. It's the worst combination behind an already-crammed set of foreground photographs. Except maybe baby pink and sky blue. Compare this poster to the simple elegance of the first two. I've just remembered that I called my section The Best of the Old School, yet all I've done is whinge. I need to find a belter to get back on track. Ladies and gentlemen, I present to you…

The Secret Rivals (1976)

Ng See-Yuen's indie epic, showcasing the talents of John Liu, Wong Tao and Hwang Jang Lee, is a huge fan favourite. Yuen Biao plays a student in another small role. The poster is a true work of art. A masterclass of considered design and understated magnificence.

Firstly, everything is painted in a masterful way, which seems to blend near-realism with gentle watercolours. I don't even know if that was the medium, but there's a subdued gentleness to the brushwork at odds with the facial expressions and action shots of the subjects. The lighting on every head is excellent, really bringing the emotions etched on their faces to life. Observe the arrangement of them, too. They are stacked like a sharp peak, facing in multiple directions, gradually getting larger as they reach the top. Yeo Su-Jin and Hwang Jang Lee engage the viewer directly, the former the love interest of our heroes, the latter the murdering antagonist. One designed to evoke sympathy, the other to threaten. Expressions are moody and serious, drawing the viewer into speculation about the motivations of each character. The action shot at the foot of the image is kinetically-charged and promises much. At the top of the page we have a beautifully-sketched mill, connected by a golden half-border to the magenta text at the bottom. It's a wonderful addition – totally unnecessary, yet it one hundred percent works. The font colours are bold, yet the size of the text doesn't overpower the artwork. It's an incredible poster and worthy of any collection. And no, I don't bloody well have one, much to my chagrin.

Snuff Bottle Connection (1977)
A Taiwanese classic, again featuring John Liu and Hwang Jang Lee in a stellar cast. Yuen Biao appears as a 'fighter in a restaurant'.
The original poster goes for high figures due to the film's cult status, and it certainly packs a punch. I've never been sure about the red and blue lines drawn vertically. What's the point of them? Regardless, the balance is good, with a dark background encouraging the two leads to stand out, presented back-to-back. The action shots in the bottom half are very well chosen, especially the lower one, which includes the immediate setting. The black above it makes it look like the duel is taking place in a silent, menacing arena. The blood-soaked title font adds to the sense of violence and mortal danger.

The Thai variant is very different. It's sketched, for starters. The vertical lines are there, but all blue. The faces look slightly 'off', even though they are taken from the same photo. There's a couple of action shots sneaked here and there, but the defining aspect of the poster is the image of John Liu kicking. His head and torso are rather good, but the legs look slightly strange. It's a difficult stance to draw, for sure, but not helped by my dislike for motion blur. Not one right foot, but five! Wow, it looks great…

Rescuing the poster entirely is the amazing selection of background colours. The red and yellow hues are lovely enough, but the real star of the show is the black and green in the top left. It's absolutely lovely.
I prefer the original poster, but the Thai variant, for all its faults, definitely has a charm of its own.

Hero of the Wild (1977)

Another fabulous background holds together this montage of photos, ably assisted by a stunning title font, which not only presents the text, but forces it from an origin point in the distance via gorgeously-shaded black lines shaded with tones of purple. Without the sunset backdrop and the title art, it's an unremarkable poster of a decent film starring Chen Sing and Hwang Jang Lee. Yuen Biao gets a higher billing this time, as a sword and knife fighter.

Of interest to readers may be the Korean variant of this poster, which is rather lovely. Everything is hand-drawn, and basks in a warmness that's very easy on the eye. The different sizes of the faces in the centre third is very effective, presenting the main characters facing in different directions, lending the piece an epic quality. The exchange in the bottom section is lively and energetic, and the montage at the top, including action shots and a panned out setting, is a nice counterpoint to the larger elements underneath. A really classy poster.

Fatal Flying Guillotines (1977)

We're back to the role of 'extra' here, in this decent little flick starring Carter Wong and Chen Sing. The original poster is pretty tricky to find. I've two versions in my collection, none of which are the Hong Kong original, but use the source. The first one I have includes a banner stuck over the original text. It doesn't detract from the poster too much, although I do feel like I'd have a cracking original if I could peel it off without ruining it, though.

The second variant I have is the Lebanese poster. It's exactly the same, but reveals more of the original design, including the arched text. The replacement of the 'e' in 'guillotines' with a 'g' continues to amuse since the day I received it. It's a super little design, with the guillotines taking centre stage – as they should! These

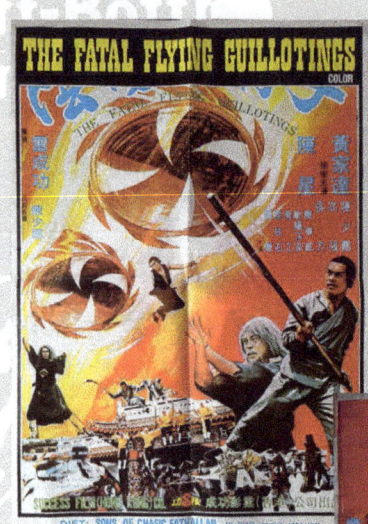

are integral to the film – unlike the lion head mentioned earlier. It's a very busy design, but the chaos is controlled, being confined to one area of the poster. There's a decent mix of photographs and artwork, with the colours creating a nice balance throughout.

And there we have it. A varied presentation of the old school, showcasing several lovely and interesting examples of poster art of films featuring Yuen Biao. Over to you, Matt. Convince me!

Educating the Ignorant

Come on Alan, they vaguely pass as Yuen Biao posters. Class movies they might be with awesome art, but they are Yuen Biao movie posters in the vaguest sense of the word. So prepare to be blown away (not literally of course) by my choices, we still need you to make me look good on here.

Righting Wrongs (1986)

First up, the action classic, 'Righting Wrongs.' Not only a corker of a movie, with brilliantly choreographed action, and knock out set pieces, but a great little poster in its own way. I am a sucker for action posters that boast a ferocious looking expression on the lead actor's face, and here it is, smack-bang in the middle of the poster. Great gritty image of Yuen Biao holding a gun with some moody blue and red colours filling up the rest of the poster. Do you see that, Alan? Yuen Biao actually on a 'Yuen Biao' poster. Fancy that!

Boom! 1-0 to Matt vs Alan.

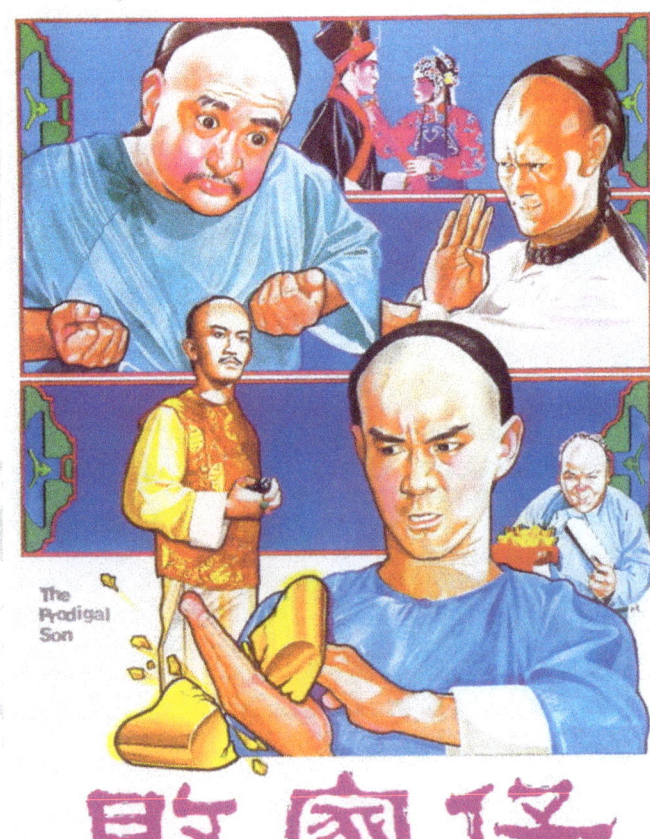

The Prodigal Son (1981)
My second poster is a genre kung fu classic, Sammo Hung's extraordinary martial arts masterpiece, 'The Prodigal Son.' I love the Hong Kong version of this poster, with its beautiful colours that really stand out well. It's like a painting, with all the main characters of the movie featured, and Yuen Biao prominently displayed in full Wing Chun pose mode, with Sammo pulling a funny-looking face. It's a poster that took me a long time to find as a collector, but I'm very relieved that I did, as it's one of my favourite Hong Kong posters. I have thrown the Thai version of the poster in the mix too. Mainly because I love the natural, hand-drawn artwork, but also just simply because Yuen Biao does a 'Drake' pose before Drake did.

2-0 with no reply here, Alan. You are not doing very well… again.

Dreadnaught (1981)

Dreadnaught is my choice for poster number 3. Not the greatest of his posters, but it's a wonderful film whereby the poster successfully captures the key images. The yellow title font stands out clearly over the dark background, with a montage of multiple shots of the stars of the movie headlining the centre. I would love to own this poster in real life, but sadly that hasn't happened yet. This film personally influenced my film-making style in so many ways. The washing scene, and the Kwan Tak-Hing clothes measuring scene, are stunning sequences that still stand the test of time today. A solid poster of one of Yuen Biao's best movies.

As a far as football scores go, this is getting like a basketball score now, Alan. It's 3 goals and no reply.

Eastern Condors (1987)

So, onto number 4. A film that needs no introduction: 'Eastern Condors'. I have so many posters of this movie it's silly. One of my personal favourite films of all time, with great fight action, mad-as-a-hatter stunts, great direction from Sammo, and top performances from the entire cast.

The Thai poster is a fantastic one: a hand-drawn montage masterpiece comprising of some of the iconic action poses from the movie, and a great image of Yuen Biao holding a machine gun. At the time, Yuen Biao's hairstyle caused more controversy than the film, but actually, with current Asian/K-pop groups being so popular with similar hairstyles, Biao's hair suddenly fits straight in. Has to be one of my favourite posters. The colours all stand out beautifully, as they are on an all-white background, with the Thai title popping out in bright red translating to 'Raw.' Yes, Raw ... I have absolutely no idea why whatsoever, but there you go. You learn something every day. But what a great English title: 'Eastern Condors.' I think that's quite safely 4-0, and it's getting embarrassing this for you, Alan. I am so sorry.

Knockabout (1979)
Moving rapidly onto my final choice, and it's another Thai poster. This time, 'Knockabout.' Not 80s, but nearly 80s, so you should love this one, Alan. Similar in style to the Hong Kong version, the Thai poster goes the extra mile and presents us with more fabulous iconic images from this all-time classic kung fu movie. Yellows, oranges and reds all combine to great effect to replace the standard white background of the Hong Kong Poster. The image of Sammo in the top right is so well drawn it looks photo realistic. There are two larger images of Yuen Biao to the centre: the classic 'laughing' Hong Kong style image, and the classic pose when Yuen Biao's character begins successfully adopting the Monkey style of kung fu in co-ordination with Sammo in the movie. The Thai title translates to 'Young Man Punching Celery.' Do not ask me what the celery did to Yuen Biao, but he obviously wasn't very happy. This movie was Yuen Biao's breakthrough role, and it's easy to see why. For one, Sammo does an amazing job in directing him, and putting him in a movie with kung fu movie stalwarts like Leung Kar Yan and Lau Gar Wing. The fight scenes crackle with life, and I absolutely love the rope training scene in the forest, where Yuen Biao gets to show off his amazing acrobatic skills. A phenomenal talent exploded onto the Kung Fu movie scene in the film, and he became a front-and-centre star. Not a background artist, like Alan seems to be celebrating.

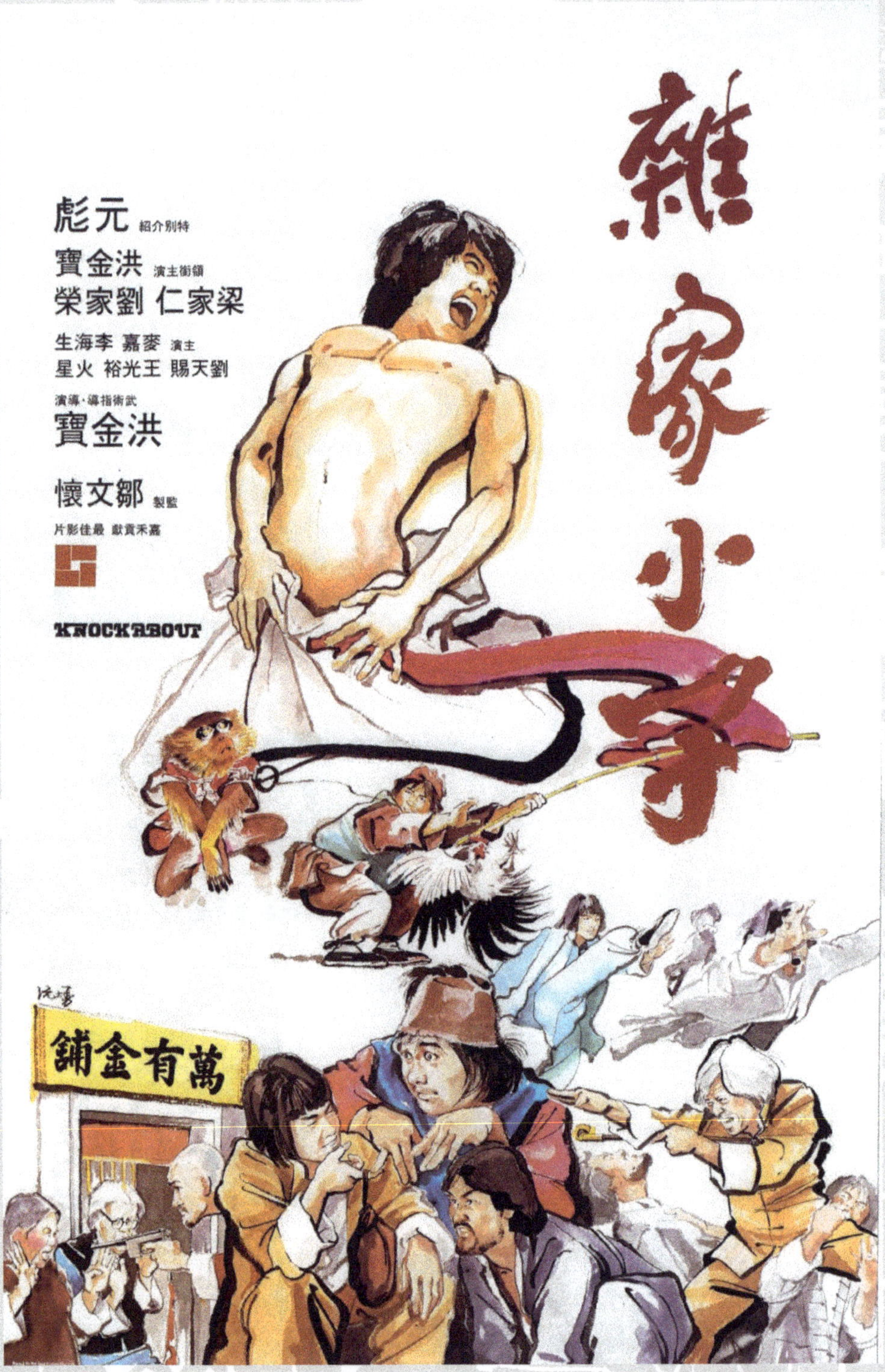

Well, there you have it. 5-0. An emphatic victory of 'Harlem Globetrotter' proportions. I think you need to go and watch some REAL Yuen Biao movies now, Alan, not excuses just to show us some awesome kung fu art. In the meantime, I am going to stick on 'Iceman Cometh' and bask in glory.

Closing Comments
AD: I think I'll set up and 'out-of-office' reply at this point to avoid fielding any awkward comments…

MR: In the duel between the old school and the more modern posters, it's a definite FATALITY!

AD: Agreed. I can't deny that your choices are more relevant, and exploit my ignorance.

MR: Everyone has to start somewhere. No more excuses. Get watching the 80s stuff. Then appreciate the poster art.

AD: I will. I set out my stall with a flimsy justification, just to shoehorn-in 1970s poster artwork, and cover up my lack of knowledge and appreciation. I still reckon most of mine are better posters than yours, but I'll maybe feel differently when I watch Yuen Biao's leading man classics.

MR: 5-0. Scorelines don't lie, Alan, and the word 'emphatic' springs to mind.

Alan Donkin & Matt Routledge

www.ingramcontent.com/pod-product-compliance
Lightning Source LLC
Chambersburg PA
CBHW051323110526
44590CB00031B/4455